The LEICESTERSHIRE & RUTLAND Cook Book

A celebration of the amazing food & drink on our doorstep.

The Leicestershire & Rutland Cook Book

©2016 Meze Publishing. All rights reserved.

First edition printed in 2016 in the UK.

ISBN: 978-0-9928981-8-2

Thank you to: Tim Hart, John Duffin
& Matthew O'Callaghan OBE

Compiled by: Lisa Pullen, Amanda Lester

Written by: Tim Burke

Photography by:
Tim Green (www.timgreenphotographer.co.uk)

Sam Bowles (www.portraitcollective.com)

Paul Carroll (www.portraitcollective.com)

Edited by: Rachel Heward, Phil Turner

Designed by: Paul Cocker, Marc Barker

Cover art: Luke Prest, www.lukeprest.com

Contributors: Kerre Chen, Kelsie Marsden,
Faye Bailey

Published by Meze Publishing Limited
Unit 1 Beehive Works
Milton Street
Sheffield S3 7WL
Web: www.mezepublishing.co.uk
Tel: 0114 275 7709
Email: info@mezepublishing.co.uk

FOREWORD

When we started to trade at Hambleton Hall in 1980 our region had limited credentials as a destination for foodies. Representation for Leicestershire and Rutland in the independent guide books (Egon Ronay, Michelin, Good Food Guide) was minimal.

One catalyst for change has been the huge increase in visitor numbers. The construction of Rutland Water in 1976 created dramatic scenery, water sports, walking and cycling possibilities and the gradual evolution of an exceptional habitat for bird life.

But visitors need nourishment and our network of pubs and restaurants has evolved to meet the need.

Back in 1980 I was always anxious that a restaurant such as our own, aiming at the very top of the market, was insecurely based if the region did not also have a strong offering in the mid-market. After all, our new clients acquire the habit of eating out in mid-market restaurants before investing in the best, and the training of chefs and waiters must be shared amongst many good places.

At the time of writing this, at least five of the best gastropubs within 15 minutes of Hambleton Hall are headed by ex-Hambleton chefs or front of house staff and I am proud that we have had a lasting impact on this arena.

Great restaurants need great ingredients. Happily we are seeing more and more small producers growing vegetables, making cheese or charcuterie or raising animals for the table. At Hambleton Bakery we have had an impact in the provision of artisan bread, cakes and savouries and we have a steady flow of visitors from outside the region for whom a bakery visit cements the region's reputation for good food.

I still sometimes envy our continental neighbours for their food traditions and great ingredients, but for game, beef, lamb, cheese and of course pork pies, we are unbeatable!

Tim Hart

CONTENTS

My food MEMORIES

Food writer Tim Burke talks about his food journey
and discovering the secrets of Leicestershire.

One of the greatest gifts a parent can give a child is the love of food. So thanks, mum. You may have grown up with rationing and poverty, and we may not have lived on a farm or even near a decent market. We weren't – dreaded term – "foodies", but you were enthusiastic about food and you were keen to expand your knowledge and skills to feed your family in the best way you could.

You supported and challenged me as a child to want to cook and to value great culinary experiences. And that has given me so much pleasure through my life – and even helped me earn a living by writing a little about food.

Stand out memories from my childhood range from rich, fudgy, nutty chocolate puddings to spicy nasi goreng – and believe me there wasn't a big Indonesian street food scene in London SE9 in the late 1960s. And then there were our summer holidays – from a summertime trip to Norway as a seven year old I remember dark, gamey reindeer and sublime halibut steaks from a fish just pulled out of a deep-water fjord, and a few years later the simple but massively enjoyable treat of simple grilled chicken and a glass of rough red wine in a Catalan fishing village.

But despite all this, when I finally pitched up in Leicester in the early 1980s it took a while to realise what a wealth of food culture we have here. Eventually I ventured up the Belgrave Road in search of the fabled Bobby's and found a wealth of vegetarian Indian cuisine I'd never even imagined on the Golden Mile. When I managed to get a car I got out to Melton Mowbray and Rutland and found not just great pork pies and cheese, but a real culture of valuing locally produced food well before it became fashionable.

As time has gone by it's been a delight to see our counties' food scene grow. We've now got Michelin stars in Rutland and Leicestershire, an improving middle-range of well-run dining pubs and an ever-growing range of cafés and restaurants from across the thrilling diversity of Leicester's communities. In all these places food and hospitality is valued both for the sensual pleasure and for its ability to bring people together.

Then of course there's our wonderful, vibrant markets and farmers and producers who really care about supplying fine produce.

There are huge opportunities out there for new and exciting food experiences and if this book encourages you and your loved ones to try some of them and to pass on that love of food – well, I'll be delighted. And so I'm sure, will my Mum.

Tim Burke

The place to
BE GIN

Super-premium gin from Leicestershire, with its own shop, bar and gin school.

Many of us do our best thinking when out for a walk, and that's how it worked for Jamie Baxter, Master Distiller at 45 West. A stroll through Burleigh Wood in Charnwood Forest got him thinking about the celebrated pairing of dandelion and burdock, along with the likes of silver birch and iris, as key botanicals for gin – and before long Burleighs Gin was born.

Since laws governing the business were liberalised there's been a flowering of creativity among a new generation of craft distillers and master distiller Jamie Baxter has been at the forefront. When fellow industry professionals Phil Burley and Graham Veitch were looking to set up their own business in 2013, he was the natural choice to develop the product. His revered status in the industry got them a 450 litre copper still in under half the usual lead time and helped get the new company 45 West off to a flying start.

Their super-premium Burleighs Gin brand has seen phenomenal success since 2014. It has three expressions, all made with the same 11 botanicals. The Signature is perfect for a G&T, while the peppery 47% Export is much beloved by bartenders for martinis and a Negroni. Also at 47% is the Distiller's Cut using a higher proportion of the more floral elements and essential in Jamie Baxter's own favourite cocktail the Martinez.

In an incredibly short period Burleighs has become a familiar sight in prestige venues around the country. Partly to build their presence in their home county, the company opened a new bottle store and sophisticated bar in St Martin's Square in the heart of Leicester in November 2015. This is a great showcase for their own and other top quality spirits and wines, and crucially gives them instant market feedback on their product.

The bar joins the company's own Gin School, located out at the distillery in Nanpantan, which uniquely among such ventures gives participants the opportunity to go through the whole distilling process and come up with their very own gin.

"The gin revival looks set to continue," enthuses Jamie Baxter, "It's young people who are fuelling the boom and influential bar tenders are attracted by the wide ranging flavour profiles. The mother's ruin image is disappearing fast and pubs are responding too. We're now promoting Burleighs at local tastings in Leicestershire pubs – I don't think that was imaginable ten years ago."

45 West's
ROSEMARY RICKEY

A refreshing herbal twist on a simple classic.

Ingredients

50ml Burleighs Distiller's Cut

20ml rosemary syrup (see below)

15ml fresh lime juice

Fever Tree soda water

1 lime, for garnish

For the rosemary syrup

A large handful rosemary leaves

300g white sugar

150ml boiling water

Method

Woody herbs are often overlooked in desserts and drinks, but they are far too flexible to be confined to the roasting tray. In this drink the rosemary – traditionally partnered with lemon but excellent with lime – provides a backbone to support the delicate, sour components and adds another dimension to the classic rickey.

To make rosemary syrup, pick fresh a large handful of rosemary leaves. In a blender or food processor, blitz the rosemary leaves with the sugar until the oils turn the sugar green. Pour over the boiling water, stir to dissolve the sugar and strain into a bottle. Allow to cool and store in the fridge.

To prepare the drink, combine the gin, syrup and lime juice in a tall glass. Add ice to the top, top up with soda and stir. Garnish with a sprig of fresh rosemary and a lime wheel.

45 West's
RED SNAPPER

A delicious spicy Bloody Mary inspired by Leicester's Golden Mile.

Ingredients

40ml Burleighs Export Strength

15ml fresh lime juice

15-35ml Snapper mix (to taste, see method)

150ml good quality tomato juice

15ml shiraz, to float

For the Snapper mix

150ml Worcestershire sauce

57ml Tabasco

30 turns black pepper

A large pinch of celery salt

2 pinches Maldon smoked sea salt

3 pinches garam masala

30ml honey

Method

In the 1940s the difference between a Bloody Mary and a Red Snapper was largely just in the name. Nowadays, red snapper refers to a Bloody Mary-style drink made with gin instead of vodka. The pepperiness and earthiness of Burleighs Export Strength is a perfect partner to the fiery spice of chilli. Cardamom seed, a principle ingredient of garam masala, is also one of the botanicals used in the distillation of the gin.

To make the snapper mix

In a jam jar, combine 150ml Worcestershire sauce, 57ml Tabasco, 30 turns black pepper, a large pinch of celery salt, two pinches Maldon smoked sea salt, three pinches of your favourite garam masala and 30ml honey. Stir thoroughly and shake well before use.

To prepare the drink, put all ingredients except the shiraz into a cocktail shaker with ice and gently roll – don't shake – back and forth until well mixed and chilled. Strain into a tall glass over fresh ice, gently float the shiraz on top over the back of a spoon, and garnish with pickled vegetables, a mini poppadom and mango chutney.

You're BEAUTIFUL

A pair of Leicestershire pubs that are beautiful by name and nature.

The idea behind the Beautiful Pubs Collective is simple - distinctive, independent pubs with their own personality and great tasting, carefully considered food and drink.

It started back in 2008 when Beautiful Pubs founder Sam Hagger took on the The Forge Inn in Glenfield. Sam is a man passionate about pubs, food and drink, and together with his team has transformed The Forge into a busy but relaxed dining pub. Its varied, innovative menu can provide something perfect for a light lunch, a Monday night supper or a weekend big night out.

After the success of The Forge, The Rutland and Derby in Leicester became the next member of the collective. The pub had become somewhat run-down but has been turned into a sophisticated city centre venue with a wide selection of craft beers, real ales and fine wines. Its menu of handmade pizzas and small sharing dishes of traditional pub items - "beer food" - is ideal for the busy local environment. It's not complicated or fussy, but it is real food with real flavour.

The Rutland and Derby was one of the first high quality, independent venues reviving the area around St Martin's. Despite being in the heart of the historical part of the city it has a splendid outdoor space, including a stylish roof garden, which is receiving further investment to create outdoor bars and a garden food offer too. It's been such a success that in its short history as a Beautiful Pub, it has already three times been awarded Leicester's Best Independent Pub by Best Bar None.

Each of these pubs may have its own unique feel that makes it just right for its environment and clientèle, but they also share the Beautiful Pubs Collective approach to high standards. All the produce that makes it onto a Beautiful Pub menu earns its place not only through flavour but through ethical sourcing too. Fish is from MSC-certified sustainable fisheries, meat is all ethically-reared, properly hung and from farms in the East Midlands, while coffee is from Rain Forest Alliance certified producers. In fact the collective's commitment to high standards made them the first independent pubs to receive accreditation through the Red Tractor quality assurance scheme.

From a warm welcome and flowers on the bar, to fine beer and tasty food – it's all about what makes a Beautiful Pub.

Beautiful Pubs Collective
PUB SCOTCH EGGS

An extremely popular favourite, enjoyed by guests in their hundreds at Beautiful Pub's city centre pub The Rutland and Derby.

Ingredients

6 large free range duck eggs

650g seasoned sausage meat (best from your local butcher, we use Owen Taylor's award-winning special sausage meat)

Handful of curly parsley, finely chopped

3 good pinches of fine sea salt and cracked black pepper

50g plain sifted flour

200g panko breadcrumbs

2 large free range hens eggs beaten, for dipping

750ml vegetable or groundnut oil, for deep frying

Method

Bring a pan of water to the boil.

Lower the duck eggs into the water and simmer for 6 minutes (for runny) 8 minutes (for set). Drain and cool under cold running water for 5 minutes. Gently tap the cooled eggs and peel the shells away and set aside. We recommend refrigerating them for half an hour.

Place the sausage meat into a bowl and add the chopped parsley, sea salt and black pepper.

Mix together thoroughly and then divide into six equal sizes balls. One at a time flatten each sausage meat ball on a roll of cling film, place the cooked and cooled duck egg into the middle of the meat and wrap around the egg, covering it evenly. Repeat with the rest of the eggs and sausage meat.

Roll each duck egg through the sifted flour, the beaten eggs and the panko breadcrumbs to coat, repeat with more egg and the panko breadcrumbs for a really even coating.

Heat the oil in a heavy-based saucepan to 150°c. Slowly lower the scotch eggs into the pan (cooking two at time) and fry for 5-6 minutes turning occasionally to colour evenly.

Remove with a slotted kitchen spoon and rest on two sheets of kitchen paper.

In the pub we serve with Stokes brown sauce but at home you could try curried mayonnaise.

Beautiful Pubs Collective
DUCK RILLETTE

A popular pub starter at The Forge Inn, prepare in advance for dinner parties but just as great for an indulgent lunch or mid-evening snack. Serves 4.

Ingredients

2 free range duck legs

300g melted duck fat

Small bunch of fresh thyme

1 large garlic clove, crushed

3 good pinches of fine sea salt & cracked black pepper

To serve

Generous amounts of toasted bread – we bake our own but if you have not got the time we recommend Pan Pugliese durum wheat bread

Cornichons (crunchy little pickles)

Chutney

Watercress

Method

Rub the duck legs with the crushed garlic and thyme sprigs and place them into a roasting tray skin side up (try and find one that fits them snugly), then pour the melted duck fat over the top.

Roast them in the oven for 2¼ hours so the meat is really tender.

Once they have cooled a little, separate the duck meat from the bones and save the juices.

Shred the duck excluding the skin, add the seasoning then separate into four small kilner jars with lids, pressing down the duck meat, then pour over a thin layer of duck fat (we actually use clarified butter in the restaurant but this is easier as you have it to hand).

Then place the jars into the fridge to chill and set.

We recommend you take them from the fridge about 30 minutes before consumption as it makes them easier to spread and also awakens the flavour a little.

Serve on the toasted bread and garnish with the cornichons, chutney and watercress.

The perfect
COUNTRY PUB

A globe-trotting pair have returned to Leicestershire to create a classic dining pub.

Lucky, lucky Wymondham. After years of the village pub changing hands on a pretty much annual basis, it was taken on by Neil and Louise Hitchen.

This Leicestershire pair had met when he was in the brigade at Hambleton Hall and she was on reception. They then spent the best part of a decade working at a variety of glamorous, top of the range restaurants in North Carolina, the British Virgin Islands, Barbados and Hampshire. When it was time to come home, the Berkeley Arms fitted their bill perfectly.

Since arriving in 2010 they established themselves purely through word of mouth as one of the finest dining pubs in the region. A Michelin Bib Gourmand came quickly and all the major guide books enthuse about both the fine cooking and the warm, friendly service.

"We've got a beautiful building and we work hard to create a friendly pub environment, not a stuffy restaurant," explains Louise. "I've taken ideas from all the fine dining places I've worked in but use them in a relaxed way. It's a great joy for me to wear jeans to work!"

The approach could be described as good British pub food, but bear in mind Neil has headed up a Michelin-starred kitchen. So the fish and chips and sausage and mash on the menu, are quite possibly the best you will come across in the region. But you may also find fillet of beef, brill delivered fresh from Brixham, technically perfect dishes such as wild rabbit and prune paté or twice-cooked cheese soufflés and stunning local game.

All chefs need good local suppliers and Neil and Louise have created a network, from villager Pam who provides their eggs to Vernon and Simon who pass on game birds from the nearby Thistleton and Stapleford shoots and Ron who shoots rabbits down on Greetham Valley golf course.

Then there's lamb from Launde, bread from Hambleton and trout from Rutland Water.

Produce like this helps but it is a passionate approach to quality and consistency that has had the reviewers purring and the diners coming back. "I think we never waiver," says Louise. "Neither Neil or I ever miss a service, which means when we have a holiday, we shut down completely."

No wonder then this village local with a chequered past is now regularly booked up with visitors from all over the region.

The Berkeley Arms
BRAISED SHOULDER OF VENISON WITH CARAMELISED WALNUTS AND POACHED PEAR

Although this dish takes 3 days to make it's well worth the wait.
Serves 6 as a main course.

Ingredients

For the venison

1 shoulder of venison

2 onions

4 carrots

1 swede

1 leek

2 bay leaves

2 celery sticks

1 bottle of red wine

Chicken stock

Salt & pepper

Flour for dusting

To make the caramelised walnuts

100g sugar

100g water

Walnuts

For the red wine poached pears

4 pears

1 bottle red wine

1 cinnamon stick

1 star anise

1 bay leaf

1 orange, zest and juice

Sugar to taste

Method

For the venison

Marinate the venison shoulder in some of the red wine and vegetables for three days.

Remove the shoulder from the marinade, reserving the liquid, season with salt and pepper and sear all over in a hot roasting tray. Remove from the roasting tray and roast the vegetables. Once the vegetables have a good caramelised colour, add more red wine and reduce by half. Place the shoulder in a roasting tray cover with the vegetables, wine and chicken stock, cover with foil and braise in the oven at 160ºc for around 3-4 hours. The meat should be tender and fall off the bone. Let the meat cool and when cool enough to touch pick the meat off the bone into a bowl and place the braised vegetables into a blender until smooth. Add to the venison meat, season with salt and pepper, add braising liquid until moist, reserving some of the sauce. Roll in cling film to form a tight roulade. Place in the fridge to firm up.

To make the caramelised walnuts

Combine the sugar and water in a saucepan. When the syrup comes to a boil, reduce the heat to a simmer, add the walnuts and cook for 10 minutes. Drain the walnuts on to an oven tray and cook in the oven for 5-8 minutes at 220ºc until caramelised.

For the red wine poached pears

Combine all ingredients in a saucepan excluding the pears. Peel the pears and quarter removing the core. Add to the wine and ingredients and bring to a slow simmer until soft.

To make the sauce

Bring the braising stock to a boil and reduce until sauce consistency. Season with salt and pepper. Strain.

To serve

Remove roulade from the fridge and cling film. Cut into 6 portions and dust with flour, sear in a hot pan with oil and butter. Place in the oven on 180ºc for 8-10 minutes until warm.

Plate up with sauce, slices of the pears and scatter with caramelised walnuts. Perfect with mashed potatoes and savoy cabbage.

Style and SUBSTANCE

Beautiful country pub and café given a new lease of life with adventurous and exciting food.

Many Leicestershire folk remember the Bewicke Arms as a thriving, characterful pub back in the 1980s. It had a fallow period but it's now roaring back as a glorious country pub combining an open and friendly approach with destination dining and its own stylish café across the courtyard.

Local boy Simon Tait remembered the good times. He had gone away to seek his fortune before moving back with wife Claire to start a family. One day, stuck in yet another M1 traffic jam, he thought there had to be a better way – and bringing back this somewhat tired pub to its former glory was a great opportunity.

Finding the right chef who matched the Taits' passion for great food wasn't easy. "But when we met Tom Cockerill – the lights just went on," says Simon. "He's intelligent, fiercely driven and with a great passion for local produce."

Tom, known to many in Leicester for his restaurant Entropy, introduced them to Glenn Cowl formerly of the Red Lion in Stathern, and the two chefs have now formed a formidable team in the kitchen. Launching in 2015, the revived Bewicke has become a magnet for food lovers looking for something a bit more interesting and exciting than most pubs in the area.

The Bewicke team are adventurous and innovative, using the very best of local produce. So you'll find free range Aylesbury ducklings from nearby Bancroft Farm, Alexanders, ramsons and wild plums foraged from the hedgerows, also apples and pears picked from neighbours' gardens in the autumn in exchange for a pint or two!

They also pride themselves on seldom-used meats such as dishes using Dexter ox heart, sweetbreads and Somerset kid, alongside more familiar staples. "The kid is amazingly popular and the ox heart has gone down brilliantly," enthuses Simon.

The Bewicke is situated among the rolling hills of South Leicestershire. It's a lovely county for walking and cycling, bringing many thirsty visitors to the pub. They also run the Hare Pie Café, a beautiful, homely space that has really taken off – with fine teas and coffee supplied by St Martin's in Leicester and cakes and food with an Italian focus reflecting Claire's family heritage.

The pub and café share a delightful open space overlooked by Hare Pie Hill, site of the locally renowned bottle kicking scramble between the villagers of Hallaton and Medbourne. This event sees some 4,000 players and spectators cram the village every Easter Monday.

"We've got a beautiful environment here," says Simon. "We've worked hard at creating a relaxed and welcoming ambience. We're delighted people are taking to it so well."

The Bewicke Arms
HERB CRUSTED HAUNCH OF VENISON, PRESSING OF ROOT VEGETABLES

This recipe uses excellent local venison from woods near Exton. Serves 4

Ingredients

4 x 250g venison haunch steaks

1 tbsp rapeseed oil

100g butter

For the herb crust

20g each of fresh tarragon, parsley, rosemary and thyme

100g butter, softened

50g bone marrow

200g Gruyère cheese, grated

150g fresh white breadcrumbs

1 tsp black peppercorns, crushed

Pressing of root vegetables

1 celeriac, 4 carrots, 1 swede, 1 sweet potato, 2 turnips – all peeled and thinly sliced

500ml double cream

For the creamed cabbage

1 head of cavolo nero

200ml double cream

50g butter

For the sauce

200ml reduced venison stock or good quality beef stock

100ml red wine

50ml Port

6 juniper berries, crushed

1 tbsp shallots, chopped

20g butter

Method

Method

To prepare the pressing, preheat the oven to 140ºc. Place the different vegetables into five separate bowls, divide the cream between each bowl, season and toss gently to evenly coat the slices. Line a large loaf tin with baking paper. Carefully layer the vegetable slices, overlapping slightly until the loaf tin is full or the vegetables are used up. Place a sheet of baking paper on top of the loaf tin and place a second loaf tin on top. Weigh down with a brick or other oven-proof heavy object and bake in the oven for 2 hours. Remove from the oven and allow to cool before refrigerating, keeping the weight on. After 4 hours, turn out the pressing onto a chopping board and cut into rectangles. When ready to serve, place the pressing back in the oven for 10 minutes to warm through.

For the herb crust, place all the ingredients into a food processor and blend until smooth, roll out between two sheets of baking paper and set in the refrigerator.

To make the creamed cabbage, finely shred the cavolo nero and boil for 5 minutes in salted water, drain well. Boil the cream and butter, reduce by half then blend in a food processor with one-third of the cavolo nero, add this cream mix back to the remaining cavolo nero, mix well and season.

To make the sauce, place all the ingredients together except the butter and reduce in a shallow pan until it begins to thicken, strain into a sauce pan and whisk in the butter over a high heat.

Season the venison steaks. In a hot frying pan, add the rapeseed oil, colour the steaks all over before adding the butter. Remove the pan from the heat and allow the steaks to rest in the butter for 5 minutes. Cut four rectangles from the herb crust and place on top of each of the steaks before placing under a hot grill for 2-3 minutes.

To assemble, place the pressing and a little creamed cabbage on each plate, slice each venison steak into two pieces and place on top of the cabbage, spoon over a little of the sauce and serve.

The Hare Pie Café
HUMMINGBIRD CAKE

No hummingbirds were harmed in the making of this cake!

Ingredients

400g self-raising flour

400g golden caster sugar

1 tsp cinnamon

3 free-range eggs

300ml sunflower oil

200g tinned crushed pineapple (use drained pieces and whizz them in a processor)

100g pecans or walnuts, roughly chopped

2 bananas, medium size, roughly mashed

For the frosting

200g soft cheese (Philly type)

125g unsalted butter, softened

250g icing sugar

1 tsp vanilla paste

To decorate

A few walnut or pecan halves

A few slithers of pineapple

Method

Heat the oven to 180ºc/fan 160ºc and line two 10 inch sandwich tins with baking parchment.

Sift the flour, sugar and cinnamon into a bowl. Add the eggs and oil, followed by the pineapple and mix. Fold in the pecans or walnuts and banana, then divide the mixture between two tins and bake for 25-30 minutes or until the cake pulls away from the edge of the tins and a skewer comes out without any cake mixture on it.

Cool for 10 minutes then turn out onto a rack, leaving the lining on, and cool completely. Meanwhile combine softened butter and icing sugar, then add the soft cheese and vanilla and beat or whisk with a hand mixer until thick and creamy. The mixture will be quite runny to start with but continue until the mixture resembles softly whipped cream. Place in fridge until needed.

Put the bottom layer, lining-side up, on a cake board or plate and carefully peel off the lining paper. Spread with half the frosting and put the remaining half on lining side up and carefully remove the paper. Frost the top of the cake and top with a few walnut or pecan halves and few slithers of reserved pineapple.

Respect
IS EVERYTHING

A fine product, with a link to our history, is now available to all.

Let's get something straight from the beginning. The deer at Bradgate Park have been culled from time immemorial. The park is a delimited space of 900 acres and hence every year around a quarter of the herd of 500 need to be culled if this unique environment is to be preserved.

But since 2013, instead of the fabulous meat from these beasts disappearing off to a few game dealers for a pittance, the meat is being made commercially available and can now be bought at some of the region's top restaurants and from selected butchers. Given that the park was given in trust to the people of Leicestershire in 1928, it seems a heartwarming and entirely appropriate development that finally this tasty, healthy and sustainably produced meat is available to the people too.

There's a world of difference between Bradgate Park venison and the farmed variety. They may frolic happily alongside the visiting hordes at the park, but these deer are classified under EU law as wild animals. They are free to range over the park and their own small reserve and are not ear-tagged, vaccinated or handled in any way. They exist on grass year round which is supplemented with hay, some extra mineral supplements and a specially formulated concentrated feed with just the right balance of nutrients to get them through the winter.

"The herd have been here for an unbroken period of 800 years," explains Bradgate Park Trust director Peter Tyldesley. "That is what made this into a Site of Special Scientific Interest, and that is what determines how we manage it. We don't want it under-grazed or over-grazed, so we cull what we need to – we'll never shoot more just because we have an order."

The light-touch and ethical husbandry of the deer is important to the Trust. They know they could probably make a lot of money by allowing commercial deer stalking but they are committed to never do that. The same person who cares for the herd will be the one to do the shooting and to prepare and package the venison.

"We have a huge knowledge of and deep respect for our deer," says Peter. "There is a bond there and welfare is very important to us."

Respect for each animal is important not least because, as Peter acknowledges, there is still a "Bambi factor" that can make people awkward about eating venison. "I always ask people who mention Bambi if they aren't vegetarian, and if they are, well fine, good for them. But if they are going to McDonalds on the way home, then there's a conversation to be had about where their food comes from!"

Deer from Bradgate Park has low food miles, low input from humans and low impact on the environment. It also has spectacular quality that has got it onto the menu of the county's Michelin-starred restaurant.

"We love supplying to restaurants because we know people will be eating it at it's best," says Peter. "Our meat has superb flavour and texture and is low fat compared to beef, but it is crucial to us that it is prepared properly. You can't just treat it like a joint of beef ."

The Trust, then, is on a mission to get more people to try venison. Some may have got the impression it is too strong and gamey for them, but when they try it, they like it. Thus whenever possible the Trust gets out the barbecue and cooks some of their burgers and sausages for park visitors. Those who want to try more can buy individual cuts at the Trust's Conservatory tea rooms in Newton Linford and from several fine butchers in Charnwood and at Leicester Market. The Trust also sells terrific value 10kg and 5kg boxes with a range of joints, steaks, casserole meat, sausages and burgers as available. The boxes also contain handy cooking tips and recipes.

There's another compelling reason to give Bradgate venison a try. While the herd has been there for 800 years, new evidence being unearthed by the University of Leicester's archaeology team suggests that local people have actually been eating red deer for some 15,000 years. In fact ever since the area was repopulated after the end of the last ice age.

"It's not just that it is great quality, eating venison offers a real link to the Bradgate story," says Peter Tyldesley. "It's not just a lump of meat, it's a piece of all our history."

Bradgate Park
KEEPER'S PIE WITH RED WINE, ROSEMARY AND GARLIC

A Bradgate twist on a classic cottage pie from Jason Bonney, Bradgate Park Ranger. Ideal for a winter week-night supper.

Ingredients

500g venison mince

Small knob of butter

3 tbsp olive oil

1 red onion

1 glass red wine

2 carrots

3 garlic cloves

1 rosemary sprig

500ml beef stock

2 tbsp beef gravy granules

1 tsp whole grain mustard

50g mushrooms (chestnut or white button)

1 celery stick (optional)

Good pinch of cracked black pepper

1kg potatoes (sweet or white or mixture of both)

Method

Begin by adding the olive oil and mince to a large saucepan. Lightly brown the mince on a medium heat then transfer to a colander to drain off any excess fat and oil.

Finely chop the onion, celery and garlic and add them with a small knob of butter to the saucepan. Allow to gently sweat for 5-10 minutes and once the onions have softened, return the mince to the pan and add the mushrooms, beef stock, red wine, rosemary and cracked black pepper. Simmer gently for 30 minutes with the saucepan lid on.

Peel and chop the carrots and add to the saucepan and continue to simmer for another 20 minutes. At this stage, you can add more vegetables such as peas, sweetcorn or broccoli to bulk the pie.

Strain the mince into a separate pan. Add 2 tbsp of gravy granules to the remaining liquid. Stir frequently on a high heat until the gravy thickens. Reduce the heat and add the mince back to the gravy and stir for 2 minutes. Transfer to a suitable dish and keep hot.

Peel and chop the potatoes and boil in a medium saucepan for 12 minutes until soft.

Mash the potatoes with a dash of milk, a heaped tablespoon of butter and the whole grain mustard. Once smooth, spread evenly across the top of the mince and score the top using a fork. Transfer to a hot grill until the mashed potato browns and is lightly crisped.

Serve and enjoy.

Bradgate Park
VENISON CASSEROLE

A hearty casserole to warm you up after a winter walk around the Park from
Bev Welch, Bradgate Park Catering Supervisor.
Serves 6.

Ingredients

250g rindless smoked bacon, chopped

1.2kg venison, diced

2 tbsp plain flour, seasoned with salt
and pepper

2-3 tbsp sunflower oil

16 shallots, peeled

2 garlic cloves, peeled and crushed

1 tsp ground mixed spice

750ml red wine

300g fresh, dried or frozen
cranberries

1 tbsp soft light brown sugar

300ml beef gravy

Method

In a flameproof casserole, cook the bacon in its own fat until crispy, then set aside.

Coat the venison in flour, add half the oil to the casserole and cook the venison in batches until browned on all sides adding more oil as necessary, then set aside.

Add the shallots and garlic and cook for 5 minutes until they start to brown, stirring occasionally.

Return the meat to the casserole and stir in the spices and the wine, slowly bring to the boil.

Reduce the heat and simmer for 1-1½ hours until the meat is tender. Stir in the cranberries, sugar and gravy and season to taste. Partially cover and simmer for a further 30 minutes or until the cranberries have softened.

Practice makes
PERFECT

Bringing high-quality, handmade chocolates to the masses.

Peter Gardner is happy to admit he's not always been passionate about chocolate. He's grown to love it, but his move into the world of high-quality handmade chocolates was an entrepreneurial one.

"I was fed up working in the licensed trade and looking for something creative to do in the food and drink sector. I realised no-one was doing nationally-branded handmade chocolate shops. So I researched the industry, started practising making chocolates and got a loan to set up a shop in Loughborough."

Now Peter speaks with a rare passion about his chosen business and is moving forward with exciting plans to train a new generation of young chocolatiers and build a franchise model for his business.

The Loughborough store was sold in 2013 and he opened Cocoa Amore in Leicester's Silver Arcade. In late 2015 he moved to much larger premises on Silver Street and his dreams are really starting to be realised. The shop offers sights, smells and a sense of theatre – customers can watch chocolates made in the window on a granite slab, from bestsellers such as Eton mess or salted caramel to more divisive specials such as marmite truffle. The shop uses chocolate by Luker, a socially and environmentally responsible company that is improving the quality of life for farmers in Colombia. Customers can

also drink hot chocolate or, as the venue is licensed, enjoy matching a glass of Port, dessert wine or porter with a favourite truffle or chocolate-tinged savoury treats.

Upstairs there's more production space but also an area for Cocoa Amore's immensely popular workshops. People can attend two-hour personalised sessions where they can get a thorough grounding in cocoa production, make their own unique chocolates and learn the skills to do more at home.

"People enjoy that but equally it's important for us to educate consumers about good chocolate and why it may cost a bit more," explains Peter. "Our products remain good value – but cheap does not always equal value for money."

When the renovation of the new building is complete, Cocoa Amore will be opening a training centre. Inspired by Jamie Oliver's 15, the business will be training young apprentices in basic skills that will help their employability in the catering industry no end. These young people could be a resource for future franchises - or maybe will take their own.

"We've worked hard to establish a reputation – we're now ready to expand," says Peter.

Cocoa Amore

SMOKED MACKEREL GANACHE WITH COCOA, TREACLE AND PORTER BREAD

Chocolate and fish? Believe it. Try this stunner as a canapé or starter.

Ingredients

For the cocoa, treacle and porter bread

2x7g yeast sachets

30g fresh yeast

800g strong white flour

50g cocoa powder

30g butter

75g treacle

50g caster sugar

150ml water, lukewarm

33cl Curious Porter

1 tbsp salt

For the Cocoa nib butter

250g unsalted butter

50g Luker Colombian cocoa nibs

10g finely grated Willie's Cacao 100% Cuban

Sea salt flakes and pepper to taste

For the smoked mackerel ganache

150g smoked mackerel

50g Luker Colombian Origin white chocolate

1 tbsp horseradish sauce

200g soft cream cheese

Juice of one lemon, along with finely-pared zest of ½ a lemon

Clarified butter to seal

Method

For the ganache

Finely shred the mackerel between your fingers, double checking that all of the bones have been removed. Add the soft cream cheese and mix together.

Add lemon juice, lemon zest and horseradish then mix again. Gently melt the Luker chocolate in a microwave using a plastic bowl. Once melted, add to the mackerel mixture and quickly incorporate before the chocolate sets. Taste and season. Spoon into ramekins and tap on a table top to release air bubbles, then seal with melted clarified butter and chill for an hour.

For the butter

Grind the Luker cocoa nibs in a pestle and mortar.

Soften the butter, then add the nibs and grated Willie's Cacao and mix.

Add salt and pepper to taste.

Cut a rectangle of cling film about 30cm x 30cm and roll the butter into a tight sausage shape and place in the fridge until needed.

For the bread

Mix yeast and warm water and leave for 3 minutes. Pile the flour and cocoa powder into a bowl and make a large well in the centre. Pour in the water, treacle and butter, then add salt and sugar and stir, then add all the porter.

Carefully bring in the flour from the inside of the well. Continue until you get a porridge-like consistency, eventually bringing in all the flour. Add a little more water if needed.

Now for the elbow grease - push, fold, slap and roll the dough around for 5 minutes until you have a silky, elastic dough. Flour the top of the dough, cover with cling film and leave to prove for half an hour until doubled in size.

Once the dough has doubled in size, knock the air out for 30 seconds by bashing and squashing it. Then leave to prove again until it has doubled in size once more. This is the most important part, as the second prove will give it the air that ends up being cooked into your bread, giving a really light, soft texture.

Preheat the oven to 180°C, and gently place your dough on a flour-dusted baking tray. Bake for 25-30 minutes until a nice crust has formed. You can tell if it's cooked by tapping its bottom – if it sounds hollow it's done. Place on a rack and allow to cool for at least 30 minutes.

We recommend serving with a crisp New Zealand sauvignon blanc or Meantime wheat beer.

Listening to their CUSTOMERS

Loughborough deli strives to find exciting, high quality,
specialist fine foods from producers with passion.

Admit it – many of you have dreamt of chucking in the day job and opening a little shop full of the food you love.

Well sisters-in-law Jenny Smith and Jane Platts are living the dream. The Deli at 58 only opened late in 2015 and has quickly established itself as a key part of Loughborough's food scene. Set in a beamed Victorian building with tons of character, the deli is packed with the finest local and national artisan cheeses, local hand-raised pork pies, cured meats, artisan breads, home made chutneys and preserves, cakes, organic vegetables, eggs and much more.

"People come in and just love the ambience," says Jenny. "They wish they could bottle the smell and take it home! A lot of our customers are really interested in food and we love to talk to them about the produce we stock."

The pair spent a good few months researching and visiting the suppliers they wanted to feature. "We really want to develop relationships with producers," says Jenny. "It's a real joy to go direct to suppliers, people who have a passion for what they produce, and to work with them on how to get the best out of it."

It's a point of principle for Jenny and Jane to try and bring exciting new products to Loughborough, especially from local independent producers, that go beyond what can be found in the supermarkets. And like any new shop they've been listening to the customers and getting in more of what people want.

So there's plenty of bread from artisan producers at the Welbeck Estate and Hambleton bakery, British charcuterie from award winning producers such as Rutland Charcuterie and Forest Pig, and even bio-dynamically grown organic vegetables from a local farmer that they also make into their popular soups.

Their lunch time trade is growing and local businesses are catching on to the quality on offer and requesting deliveries for lunches and meetings. In future they hope to be able to create some outside space for people to sit and enjoy a coffee or maybe even a glass of wine through a link up with their neighbouring wine merchants.

"This is just what Loughborough needed," said one happy customer early on. "It's the kind of place that everywhere needs."

COLSTON BASSETT
AND SPRING ONION SCONES

A savoury treat made with local cheese. Makes 15 scones.

Ingredients

450g self-raising flour

3 tsp baking powder

Salt, large pinch

3 spring onions, chopped

50g butter

300g Colston Bassett Stilton

284ml milk, approximately

Method

Put the flour, baking powder and salt in a basin.

Rub in the butter, until the mixture resembles fine breadcrumbs.

Stir in 225g of the cheese, the chopped spring onions and sufficient milk to give a soft, manageable dough.

Knead gently, then roll out the dough to 2.5cm thickness.

Stamp out 7.5 cm rounds with a fluted cookie cutter.

Brush with milk and sprinkle with the remaining cheese.

Bake in the oven at 200ºc for around 20 minutes until golden.

Cool on a wire tray and serve.

You can bank
ON DELILAH'S

One of the UK's great delis is now in Leicester too.

Sangita Tryner speaks with a rare passion; not least because she's trying to get across the dedication of the producers of the goods that pack her extraordinary deli, Delilah. It's an Aladdin's cave of the very finest foods.

"I listen to producers talking about their products, and the passion is there to taste in every mouthful," says Sangita. "Our job is to make sure that our customers get to share that experience. That's why we want people to get up close and personal to the food – we don't hide our cheese behind glass, we want you to get so close you can almost taste it."

Many Leicestershire folk know Delilah from visits to Nottingham, so the news that they were to open a branch in the heart of Leicester in late Spring 2016 sent a huge buzz around the foodie community. The Leicester shop, located in the old Allied Irish Bank in St Martin's, has all the things that makes the multi-award winning Nottingham store so beloved.

The building is stunning, a faithfully restored Victorian neo-Gothic banking hall, with a wealth of original features: a double-height ceiling provides space for a mezzanine dining area, while the ground floor houses the extensive deli and the popular seated bar area.

Delilah's kitchen team assemble food ranging from cake and coffee to full meals, using the cornucopia of top quality cheeses, meats, breads, pickles, preserves and more in the store. A typical dish might be heritage and pickled beetroot with toasted walnuts, ash-coated goat's cheese and local honey.

Dishes can be complemented by a choice from the 200 fine wines on sale, sourced by Sangita's wine buyer-husband mostly from small, owner-producers, and focusing heavily on dynamic up-and-coming regions. Any of the wines can be 'drunk in' for a small corkage charge, and there is a constantly changing range available by the glass.

"We're huge fans of East Midlands produce, as well the best of British and international," adds Sangita, who cites London's legendary Villandry in its hey-day as her inspiration. "There's a story to tell behind everything we sell, but the proof of the pudding is in the eating, and we encourage sampling and tasting. We really want you to try the products that we love - that's what Delilah is all about.

"Bringing this lovely building back to life is so satisfying," she concludes. "and I've never seen a city change so fast – Leicester is just so exciting right now!"

Delilah's
SWISS CHEESE FONDUE
SERVED WITH CRUDITÉS

A really easy dish to recreate at home with regular kitchen equipment. The three cheeses are selected to bring savoury, fruity and creamy elements to the dish, while you can be as imaginative as you like in your choice of what to dip.

Serves 2

Ingredients

For the fondue

100g grated Emmental cheese

60g grated Appenzellar cheese

100g grated Gruyère cheese

1 garlic clove

125ml white wine

1 tbsp plain flour (or cornflour for a gluten-free option)

For the crudities

1 carrot, cut into strips

1 fig, chopped

200g boiled new potatoes

40g cherry tomatoes, halved

¼ cucumber, cut into the finger shaped strips

80g Rosette salami (or other), cut into chunks

150g Alderton marmalade ham, sliced thick & cut into chunks

1 sourdough bread, sliced thick & cut into chunks

1 celery stick, cut into bite size pieces

A handful of grapes

Method

Peel the garlic clove and then holding it between your fingers, rub the base and the sides of a saucepan with the clove.

Add the wine to the pan and place on a medium heat.

Once simmering add all of the grated cheese to the pan and stir continuously until all the cheese has melted – leave on the heat on a slow simmer.

In a small bowl mix the flour with a splash of cold water to create a smooth and thick paste and then slowly stir the paste into the cheese mixture.

This will thicken and emulsify the cheese mixture, (the fondue should coat the back of a spoon).

Pour the fondue into your favourite pot and serve immediately alongside the crudités for a decadent dip!

Delilah's
FRENCH TOAST

The important thing here is the quality of the bread – real artisan bread absorbs the egg without turning to mush – using the right pancetta to get a crispy, salty, smokey kick; and using a good maple syrup, not a "maple-flavoured" alternative. Serves 1.

Ingredients

4 slices of Hambleton Bakery French Baguette, cut at an angle to get a larger surface area

1 free range egg

4 or 5 thinly sliced rashers of pancetta stesa (lightly smoked)

30ml good quality maple syrup

30g unsalted butter

Splash olive oil

Method

Preheat your grill.

Place a frying pan on a medium heat with the knob of butter and a splash of olive oil (so the butter doesn't burn).

Whisk the egg in a mixing bowl and then dip the 4 slices of baguette in the whisked egg mixture until the bread is completely coated and has absorbed most of the egg.

Add the eggy bread slices into the now hot frying pan and cook the bread on both sides until golden brown.

While the French toast is cooking in the frying pan, line up the pancetta slices on a baking tray and place under the grill. Cook until crisp and brittle.

Place the French toast onto a plate, arrange the pancetta over the top and finally drizzle the maple syrup over.

The proof is in THE PIE

Melton's longest established pork pie makers are the guardians of a noble tradition.

John Dickinson may not have been the very first pie maker in Melton Mowbray, but the fact that after 165 years his shop still thrives suggests he was one of the best.

Ye Olde Pork Pie shop in Melton is the site of his original bakehouse and the pork pie business he built up with Joseph Morris. Today it sells 3,000 pies a week - ten times that figure in the run up to Christmas - with baking still done from 2am, six days a week. With some 30 per cent of customers being visitors to the town it is a major tourist attraction and a key part of Melton's status as England's Rural Capital of Food.

In these days when the British have started to value provenance in food, the story of how Melton Mowbray became synonymous with quality pork pies is worth telling, and Stephen Hallam, managing director of Dickinson and Morris is the man to tell it.

"There was a lot of cheese made in the Vale of Belvoir, and the by-product whey was a good food supplement for pigs," he explains. "The surplus of pork that resulted meant it became a standard lunch for the local rural labourers. At that time though they would crudely wrap a hunk of meat in pastry and put it the fire, throwing away the pastry 'coffin'."

During the winter months the agricultural labourers would work for the hunts, and the hunting folk took a shine to this humble fare. It was John Dickinson's grandma, explains Stephen, who made them into a more refined version with pastry to be eaten and jelly to protect the pie while they bumped around in saddlebags.

The fame of these pies spread and the name of Melton Mowbray would be forever linked. Today at Ye Olde Pork Pie Shoppe, Dickinson and Morris has other specialities too – from hand-linked sausages and artisan bread baked on site, to Melton Hunt Cake, a rich, moist fruitcake still made to the recipe developed by Joe Morris for the hunting folk to enjoy with their stirrup cup.

"People increasingly have a real desire to seek out better quality food with heritage," says Stephen Hallam. "We are proud so many people make a pilgrimage to find us and learn about the fascinating link between Melton Mowbray, pork pies and stilton cheese – and of course to sample some pie!"

YE OLDE PORK PIE SHOPPE

PORK PIES

PORK PIES

DICKINSON & MORRIS
OF MELTON MOWBRAY
SINCE 1851

Dickinson and Morris
PORK PIE

Here's how you can make a 1kg pork pie of your own at home.

Ingredients

For the pastry

112g plain flour

½ tsp salt

50g lard

32ml milk and water mixed – (the milk is optional)

Beaten egg, to glaze

For the filling

225g lean pork, chopped

Salt and pepper

5 tbsp pork stock

15g gelatine

Method

To make the pastry

Sift the flour and salt into a warm bowl and rub in 15g of lard. Gently heat the remaining lard, water and milk together until boiling, then add to the flour, mixing with a wooden spoon until the mixture is cool enough to knead by hand. Knead well. Reserve a quarter of the pastry for the lid. Shape the remaining piece into a round dome and leave both overnight in the fridge.

To raise the pie

Remove the pastry from the fridge a couple of hours before making the pie case. Gently temper the pastry by squeezing between both hands so that it becomes pliable. Using your hands carefully mould the pastry up and around a wooden dolly (or floured jam jar), ensuring that the sides are of an even thickness. Remove the pastry case from the jar.

For the filling

Chop the pork and season with salt and pepper. Place the pork filling into the pastry case. Roll out the pastry for the lid, damp the rim of the pastry case with egg and press together. Brush the top of the pie (not the crimp) with egg and make a hole in the centre of the lid. Chill thoroughly, preferably overnight.

Baking the pie

Bake in a hot oven 220ºc for approximately 1½ hours. When baked, remove from oven and allow to slightly cool.

Jellying

Whilst the pie is baking make the jelly by dissolving the gelatine in some pork stock. Make two holes in the lid of the pie and pour in the jelly. After jellying place the pie in a fridge until the jelly has set, preferably overnight.

Eating!

The pork pie is designed to be eaten cold but to enjoy it at its best, remove the pie from fridge at least an hour before eating.

From field TO FORK

An award-winning farm shop that offers a new way – which is actually the old way – of bringing fresh food to the consumer.

Growing food is Kevin Stokes' passion, and that's why he started Farndon Fields back in 1983. He was also fired by a desire to find a better way of getting fresh produce to the customer.

Selling direct from the field and creating supportive relationships with other local farmers seemed a great format for a sustainable, local business. Now, 33 years after setting up a table in the farmhouse garage, Farndon Fields is one of the biggest and best farm shops in the country and offers a real alternative to the supermarkets.

This family concern has grown steadily by reinvesting in new facilities but it still has farming at its heart. Potatoes were always the key crop but the farm has expanded along with the shop and they now grow and sell over 40 varieties of fruit and vegetables including family favourites like broccoli, beetroot and leeks. In the summer the real draw for customers is their strawberries, arguably the sweetest and juiciest in Leicestershire, and all grown in fields behind the shop. With Kevin's wife Milly bringing her interior designer's eye to the layout, it's a real foodie experience.

But there is far more than just greengrocery. Their butchery department has grown over the past 10 years and sources its meat from local farmers. The free range lamb is reared in Theddingworth by farmer Michael Skinner and beef comes directly from several neighbouring farms.

Farndon Fields is now a one-stop destination. There's bread from Hambleton Bakery, cakes handmade on site, an exquisite deli counter and a growing selection of ready prepared food – many made using the farm's own produce.

In the popular Farmer's Kitchen, chefs prepare a range of light snacks, cakes and full meals cooked fresh to order and using produce from the farm and the shop.

"We attract a wide range of customers," explains Nicola Stokes, marketing manager. "From those who pop in after work to those who do their big weekly shop here, not least because they are interested in where their food comes from."

It's no surprise the Stokes' have won numerous awards for their commitment and achievement in promoting local food. By cutting out the middle man, they can pay a fair price for their milk, for example, and to dairy farmers they know personally.

"We believe our farm shop is good for our customers and good for farmers," says Nicola. "We are very proud of what we are doing here."

Farndon Fields

WELCOME TO FARNDON FIELDS

Market Harborough

Farndon Fields
DAUPHINOISE POTATOES

A classic indulgent dish which you can dress up or down. Serves 4.

Ingredients

1kg Farndon Fields Wilja potatoes

250ml double cream

150g goat's cheese

1 onion, sliced

2 garlic cloves

1 sprig of rosemary

1 sprig of thyme

1 bay leaf

1 tsp butter

Sea salt & pepper

Method

In a heavy-bottomed saucepan combine the cream, sliced onion, garlic, rosemary, thyme, bay leaf, salt and pepper (to taste). Heat to a simmer until the cream has reduced slightly, this should take 10-15 minutes. Whilst it's simmering, peel the potatoes and slice thinly.

Next crumble up the goat's cheese and add to the cream mixture, stirring until the cheese has melted. Once melted, strain the mixture to remove the garlic, onions and herb sprigs.

Grease an ovenproof dish with a little butter before laying out some of the slices of potato to cover the bottom of the dish. Add a spoonful of the cream mixture on top. Repeat layering the potatoes and cream until you have used them all up.

Cover in tin foil and bake in the oven at 160°c for an hour. After 40 minutes, remove the tin foil to allow the top to turn golden brown. To check if it is cooked, push a knife through the potatoes. If the knife slides in easily then the potatoes are cooked.

Farndon Fields
MILLY'S WINTER SALAD

Full of Farndon Fields fresh produce, this seasonal salad will warm you up during the winter months. Serves 4.

Ingredients

300g Farndon Fields celeriac

300g Farndon Fields beetroot

300g Farndon Fields pink fir apple potatoes

150g Farndon Fields curly kale

2 mini individual goat's cheese

1 tbsp plain flour

1 free range egg, beaten in a bowl

4 tbsp breadcrumbs

1 bottle of Farndon Fields house dressing

Olive oil

Sea salt and pepper

Method

Firstly peel the celeriac and beetroot, then chop into cubes approximately 2cm square. Place them in a bowl and drizzle with olive oil and season with salt and pepper before tossing to make sure they are fully covered. Next, spread them out on a baking tray and roast at 180°c for 40 minutes, or until soft in the middle and crunchy on the outside. Whilst these are roasting, scrub the pink fir apple potatoes and boil whole, with their skins on, for 20 minutes.

Cut the two goat's cheeses in half then dust each piece in flour. Next dip them into the beaten egg and roll in the breadcrumbs until fully coated. Place the coated goat's cheese on a plate and put in the fridge until you need them.

Heat a frying pan with about a half centimetre of oil in it. In the meantime strip the kale from its stalks. When the oil is hot put the kale in quickly, be warned it will spit in the first 10 seconds, stir the kale round the pan with a long handled spoon to avoid the spitting. After about 20 seconds the kale will be cooked, remove from the pan and place on some kitchen paper to soak up the remaining oil.

Once the potatoes are cooked, remove from the water and let them cool slightly. When they are ok to touch, slice into rounds about 1cm thick and fry in the oil. Once they are a lovely golden colour, remove from the pan and place on some kitchen paper. Finally, fetch the cheese from the fridge and fry in the oil until golden brown on all sides.

To assemble the dish, place the cooked celeriac, beetroot and pink fir apple potatoes in a bowl and add a generous swig of Farndon Fields house dressing. Mix around before tipping into a large bowl. Add the crispy kale and top with the breaded goat's cheese. Add some more dressing if you wish and enjoy!

The hunt for GREAT FOOD

Hotel and restaurant in Exton, Rutland, with food based on a passion for flavour and great local produce.

When Rochelle Bushell saw Rutland and the sublimely pretty village of Exton, it was love at first sight. The village had a beautiful inn just crying out for love and attention, and Rutland was ripe for something completely different. With a number of successful bars, restaurants and guest houses already under their belt in Cape Town, she and her son David Graham, had a new project.

So the Fox and Hounds opened in the summer of 2015 and, under Chef Patron David Graham, is carving a high-quality niche in Rutland's dining scene.

"There's a great sincerity in what we do; a nostalgia even," he explains. "There's a recognition that food is more than just what you put in your mouth, so we are exploring things that have a deeper meaning for us."

The result is deeply desirable dishes that come across as grown up comfort food presented with delicacy and flair. The likes of free range pork loin in yoghurt, rosemary and maple marinade, with apple purée, woodland mushrooms, pork air and cider and mustard jus.

David is also keen to return an element of theatre: "So with our scallops and artichoke for example, a velouté is poured at the table and the dish is rejuvenated. People love it, but there's a whole generation who have missed out on this kind of thing."

With the interior of the building giving a whole new meaning to dining and drinking out, David had to find a head chef who shared his and Rochelle's approach. Enter, Omar Palazzolo, a young Milanese chef who had settled in the area, but had been commuting to London to work in some of the capital's top venues.

"You could see the light in his eyes – it showed his passion," David enthuses. Omar had honed his skills at Michel Roux's two Michelin-starred La Gavroche. But he's a curious chef, and broadened his horizons at the equally iconic Nobu. Now he's fallen in love with great British produce and, at the Fox and Hounds, has been fusing all his experience with the passion for good food he and David share.

That means almost everything has its marinade, cure or something to take it up a level. Their approach also requires fabulous ingredients, and David and Omar are loving the process of sourcing the best. They are especially excited by the supplies from Ray Camplejohn, a proper old-school Leicestershire butcher: "The quality and consistency is the best I've ever come across and that is fundamental to our cooking," says David.

"We do food to eat!" adds Omar with a smile. "Good looking? Sure, but created with a passion for flavour."

Fox and Hounds

MONKFISH WITH MADRAS, VERMOUTH AND GRANNY SMITH VELOUTÉ

Serves 4.

Ingredients

1 tsp flatleaf parsley, chopped

Zest of 1 lemon

900g monkfish, cut to 4 equal portions (your fishmonger can do this for you)

12 thin slices unsmoked prosciutto

1 tbsp vegetable oil

Salt and pepper

For the Madras, Vermouth and Granny Smith velouté:

50g butter

5 shallots, thinly sliced

4 Granny Smith apples peeled, cored and thinly sliced

1 bunch coriander

1 tbsp Madras powder

1 tsp turmeric

250ml Vermouth (Martini Bianco ideally)

750ml vegetable stock (the best you can get)

500ml double cream

2 limes, zested and juiced

Salt and pepper

Method

For the velouté

Add the butter to a pan with a lid and sweat down the shallots over a medium heat. Make sure they don't catch on the pan or colour. Add the apple and half the coriander. Mix well and then add the madras and turmeric. Deglaze the pan with the Vermouth. Reduce by half and then add the stock and the cream. Simmer for 15 minutes and then add the rest of the coriander. Remove the pan from the heat and cover with cling film and leave to infuse for 15 minutes. Strain the sauce through a chinois or sieve. Blend the sauce with lime zest and juice.

For the fish

Mix the parsley and lemon zest. Season the monkfish with salt and pepper and then roll it in the mixture. Lay out two sheets of cling film, overlapping them so they easily cover your fish. Lay out three slices of prosciutto, overlapping them slightly. Place a piece of the seasoned monkfish in the middle and fold the prosciutto over the monkfish to cover it.

Tightly roll the cling film around the fish and prosciutto, making sure not to get cling film caught between the fish and the prosciutto. Grabbing the ends of the cling film, keep rolling the package on your work surface until you have a tight parcel. Tie a knot in each end. It sounds more complicated than it is – there are a number of YouTube tutorials if you need help. Repeat a further three times. Chill in the fridge for 1 hour.

Preheat the oven to 200°c. Heat the oil in a pan and remove the monkfish from the clingfilm. Brown the monkfish parcels on all sides until golden. Transfer to the hot oven for 7-8 minutes to finish cooking. Let it rest for 3-4 minutes.

Serve with the velouté and your choice of seasonal vegetables. Bok choi and yellow courgette work wonderfully, as do a handful of steamed mussels.

Chilled to PERFECTION

Glorious gelato made the artisan way with Italian passion
and Leicestershire milk.

Some people shook their heads when Daniele Taverna and Antonio De Vecchi opened an artisan gelato shop. In Leicester? With our winters?

But two years on, the sheer brilliance of their product has created an all-year-round market where none existed.

Gelato is very dear to the heart of Italians, so don't call it ice-cream – it uses more milk and less cream and sugar. But even in Italy you will find gelato made from pre-mixes, a long way from the purity and quality at Gelato Village, where the commitment to all-natural, finest quality ingredients is what drives them on.

Central to this of course is the dairy element – magnificent milk from the Red Poll herd of Leicestershire farmers Alan and Jane Hewson of Belvoir Ridge Creamery.

"Our relationship with suppliers is fundamental, and this milk gives an excellent taste," says Antonio. "We've had professional gelato makers come here from Italy and they are amazed."

Antonio adds no emulsifiers, preservatives or colourings, just natural stabilisers and seasonal flavours. That means small batch manufacturing and everything must go in three days, ensuring it is only ever sold in tip-top condition.

"We make it the Italian way, but naturally it takes on a local character," adds Daniele. "The berries we get here are much better than anything in Italy." Big hit flavours included a rose-scented berry concoction in honour of Richard III and a mango lassi that delighted Leicester's Asian community in particular. But gelato has its traditional flavours, so as well as using the best local produce, they also import perfect pistachios from Sicily and heavenly hazelnuts from their home province of Piedmont for their chocolate gianduia.

Their café in St Martin's Square is redefining the way Leicester eats out. Obviously it's a rare treat on a hot day, but the continental ambience is a big draw for those looking for an alternative to the pub, and the place does a great trade on weekend evenings in the winter too. The word is spreading with regular visits from Birmingham folk and others pleading with them to open in Manchester.

But for now IT guy Daniele and former nurse Antonio are just delighted that Leicester has responded so positively to their passion. "Our biggest reward," says Daniele, "is when we see the look on the face of someone trying true gelato for the first time."

Hart AND SOUL

Hugely revered hotel and restaurant that has also now fostered the best bakery in the UK.

Hambleton Hall has been a beacon of excellence for Rutland and Leicestershire for some 36 years. Not only has it held a Michelin star for 34 years continuously - the longest of any restaurant in the UK - but it has trained and inspired a generation of chefs and front of house staff who have gone on to run their own high quality venues in the region.

Owner Tim Hart says he was inspired by the Relais et Châteaux network in France to create a pioneering country house hotel that offered international standards of accommodation and food in a rural setting. Having made an immediate impact by gaining a Michelin star after only two years, Hambleton Hall has impressed with its consistent brilliance.

"In this time we've only had three head chefs," says Tim Hart. "The brilliant young Nicholas Gill, then Brian Baker [now of the Marquess of Exeter in Lyddington] and Aaron Patterson who joined us as an apprentice.

"Restaurants are usually run by very young people," he continues. "Many of our key staff have grown up with us and have been here 25 years or more and gained a great depth of experience - it's a huge advantage for us."

Hambleton Hall may have an international reputation but, stresses Tim Hart, the people of Leicestershire and Rutland are very important to them. Each year they serve some 12,000 lunches for an almost entirely local clientele, attracted by the exceptional food, the beautifully decorated Victorian country house surroundings and top-end service from staff who are trained to listen, understand and respond to the needs of guests.

In recent years the Hambleton name has become even more widely known through its extraordinary, influential bakery – which won the ITV programme to find "Britain's Best Bakery".

Hambleton Hall chef Julian Carter came from ten generations of bakers and wanted to do for bread what CAMRA had done for real ale in this country. Tim Hart was keen to back him and together they established a bakery in the Rutland village of Exton, which now supplies shops and restaurants across the region. Julian already had family recipes for cakes and breads and they researched more, rediscovering the likes of manchet, a rich breakfast bread that was a British predecessor to the likes of croissant and brioche.

The pair are justly proud of how they have helped change the culture of bread when they now see farmer's markets full of craft bakery stalls and even the supermarkets selling sourdough loaves.

Hambleton Hall

HAMBLETON

TON BAKED

Hambleton Hall
PLOUGHMAN'S PARCEL

Makes 20 small parcels.

Ingredients

650g strong bread flour

30g semolina

420ml warm water at 27ºc

70ml olive oil

10g sugar

20g fresh yeast (or 15g dried yeast)

Mixed seeds for the topping

2 Granny Smith apples, chopped

4 sticks of celery, chopped

360g Red Leicester cheese, grated

140g chutney

Method

Mix together the flour, semolina and sugar. Add the yeast to warm water and mix in, add the liquid to the dry ingredients and mix to a paste.

Leave to stand for twenty minutes, then knead the dough with the salt until elastic. Place in an oiled bowl and cover with a tea towel, leave until doubled in size. Tip out on to a floured table and cut into twenty 60g pieces, round into dough balls and leave to rest on the floured table, for ten minutes.

Make your filling by mixing your chopped apple, celery, Red Leicester cheese and chutney of your choice.

Place your filling in the centre of your dough ball and bring the sides of the dough around the filling to make a purse then seal the ends.

Turn them over, spray with water and dip in your seeds.

Place on a baking tray with non-stick parchment. Bake in a preheated oven at 180˚c, for 10 to 15 minutes, they should be golden brown.

As an extra treat put some more cheese on top just before you bake them.

A home from home
AT JAMES'

A relaxed café with a vintage style, providing freshly made food
and a refuge from the city crowds.

"Hidden gem" might be something of a cliché, but that's the phrase that springs to mind about James' Café Bistro. Its location – a few steps from the Clocktower, but tucked away on East Bond Street near the back entrance to Highcross – is definitely part of its charm. It's a little oasis of calm, with a quirky, vintage interior and simple, freshly-prepared and well-thought out café food in a family-friendly environment.

It might have seemed a brave move when chef James Gordon and front of house manager Debbie Oloye opened the café some five years back. The credit crunch was biting but the pair - who worked together at a Clarendon Park bistro - were aware that lunchtime trade was holding up well. A city centre venue providing lunches, coffees, cakes and snacks to hungry shoppers and office workers – plus Saturday night special events – seemed a viable option.

Key to their success has been their focus on fresh, locally-bought produce. Every day James makes the short walk to Leicester market and gets whatever's good. "People want freshness and they know they'll get that from us," says James. "If it's a simple tomato and mozzarella salad, they'll get the best tomatoes available on that day. It's such a big market – there's plenty of scope to choose."

There are different menus available over the course of the day, but James and Debbie reckon that almost a third of their business is from regulars who ask for whatever they fancy – and because of the focus on freshly-prepared food, they can generally get it.

There's something of a Mediterranean slant to the food, but traditional English food and Asian influences show up too. "Our vegetarian and vegan customers love our sweet potato and spiced chick pea cakes," say James. "It's one dish I couldn't take off the menu - vegetarians want more than just a cheese sandwich."

James' first love as a chef is desserts and all the cakes, tarts, tortes, ice-creams and sorbets are made on the premises. His chocolate brownies are another ever-present offering on the menu.

The café is a spacious one and part of it is given over to families – with high chairs and a wide variety of activities to keep kids happy while parents can enjoy their meal. It's all part of creating an escape from the hurley burley of the city centre. A place of simplicity, but of quality and character too.

James' Café Bistro

NEW James Deli
Cooking Sauces & Preserves
Take the taste home!

James' Café Bistro

LEMON TORTE WITH STRAWBERRY AND HONEY SORBET

Debbie's favourite! Something to enjoy in a great British heatwave. Serves 8.

Ingredients

For the pastry

125g salted butter

255g plain flour

30g icing sugar

1 medium free range egg

Zest of 1 medium lemon

For the filling

Zest of 2 medium lemons

Juice of 3 medium lemons

250g caster sugar

5 medium free range eggs

290ml double cream

For the sorbet

500ml puréed strawberries (ripest local ones preferred)

100g honey (locally made preferable)

400ml water

Method

For the pastry

Dice the butter and add to the flour, then rub with fingers until it resembles breadcrumbs. Mix in the icing sugar and lemon zest then add the egg and bring the mixture together to a ball, but don't overmix. Flatten slightly, wrap in cling film and refrigerate for 20 minutes. Once chilled, roll the pastry between two sheets of cling film to the desired thickness. Remove top layer of film and turn the pastry into a deep-sided, greased, floured, springform tin. Using the remaining layer of cling film push the pastry into the edges of the tin and up the sides – this will avoid it sticking to your fingers. Remove cling film and push pastry gently up the sides with fingers till its 2mm above tin to allow for shrinkage during baking. Refrigerate for 20 minutes.

Bake blind using baking parchment and pastry beans for 10 minutes at 190°c or until the edges are slightly golden. Remove the parchment and beans. If there are any cracks appearing fix them now with any spare pastry and by brushing with egg – the lemon mixture is thin and will find these cracks and cause havoc. Bake for a further 10 minutes at 180°c or until nicely crisp. Cool slightly.

For the filling

Thoroughly mix the lemon zest in to the caster sugar. In a separate bowl squeeze the lemon juice then crack in the eggs. Mix a little, then add the double cream. Stir through gently, then sieve this mixture on to the zesty sugar. Gently stir until sugar is combined. Now pour this mixture into the pastry case. This is easier if the case is already on a baking tray in the oven – it avoids carrying the liquid filled case and potential spillages. Bake at 160°c for 30-40 minutes. Cook until there's a slight wobble in the middle but no raising at the edges and no browning. Cool completely before popping out of the tin.

For the sorbet

Blend and sieve the fresh strawberries. Stir in honey and then the water. Chill for 30 minutes. Churn in an ice cream machine for 20 minutes or until soft set. If you don't have an ice cream machine place a bowl in a freezer and beat with a whisk every 15 minutes until smooth and scoopable (this may take a couple of hours).

Take a big slice of the lemon torte and scoop on the sorbet. Eat quickly in the sunshine.

John's House

BRADGATE PARK FALLOW DEER, SMOKED BEETROOT, QUINCE AND CHOCOLATE

John's House opened in 2014 on the family farm in Mountsorrel, Leicestershire. Bringing together all of his experience at the head of his own restaurant the menu at John's House changes with the seasons, and John Duffin champions a 'farm to plate' philosophy, sourcing local, British ingredients, many of which originate on the family farm. They gained their first Michelin star in 2015.

Ingredients

4 x 150g venison loin

Salt and pepper

Oil and butter for frying

For the quince

2 ripe quince

Zest of 1 lemon and 1 orange

500ml sugar syrup

1 cinnamon stick

For the pickled beetroot

2 red beetroot

50g sherry vinegar

Zest of 1 lemon

50g brown sugar

For the Savoy cabbage

1 Savoy cabbage

50g butter

Salt and pepper

For the chocolate ganache

50g dark chocolate (70%)

50ml double cream

1 tbsp raspberry vinegar

For the smoked beetroot sauce

2 large red beetroot

40g sugar

25ml raspberry vinegar

Hay for smoking

To garnish

Beetroot leaves

Method

For the beetroot sauce

Dice the beetroot into 1cm dice, lay them on a perforated tray with another deep tray underneath and put two handfuls of nice hay in the bottom tray. Have a roll of cling film at the ready. Light the hay until it has a good flame (in the garden preferably) then put the tray of beetroot on top and cover with the cling film.

Leave this to smoke for an hour. Put the smoked beets through a juicer and add the sugar and vinegar and reduce until you have a shiny sweet and sour sauce.

For the quince

Make a simple sugar syrup with equal quantities of sugar and water then add the cinnamon and zests, peel and quarter the quince, gently poach until soft, leave to cool in the liquid.

For the pickled beets

Peel the beets and boil in salted water for 30 minutes until just cooked, leave to cool.

In a separate pan, add the vinegar, sugar and lemon. When the beets are cool thinly slice and add to the sugar and vinegar mix and leave to pickle.

For the savoy cabbage

Remove the core from the cabbage and separate into individual leaves, discard the dark outer leaves. Cook the leaves in salted boiling water until well cooked, strain and chill in iced water, squeeze out as much water as possible, chop the cabbage and leave to one side.

For the chocolate ganache

Bring the cream up to the boil and pour over the chocolate, then whisk until all the chocolate has melted. Add a pinch of salt and the vinegar, then leave in the fridge to set.

To serve

Take the venison out of the fridge one hour before you plan to cook it. Season with salt and pepper and roast in a hot pan with oil and butter. When cooked how you like it leave covered in a warm place for 15 minutes to rest.

Reheat the cabbage in a pan with the butter, salt and pepper.

Reheat the quince in the syrup. Gently warm the beetroot in the pickling mixture.

When the deer is well-rested, slice thinly and arrange on four plates. Make a quenelle of the cabbage mixture, add the poached quince to the plate along with the sliced pickled beetroot.

To one side on the plate, add a quenelle of the chocolate ganache.

Reheat the smoked beetroot sauce and add nicely to the plate.

Garnish with beetroot leaves and serve.

Where tradition
MEETS QUALITY

Serving up thrilling dishes from the South Indian state of Kerala, Kayal has expanded horizons for lovers of Indian food.

Over the last 50 years Britons have developed a strong concept of what makes an "Indian restaurant". Leicester's Kayal is one of the restaurants that can honestly claim to have broken the mould.

Yes there had been a few restaurants in London serving South Indian food, but until Kayal came along none with the décor, atmosphere and style of a genuine Keralan village restaurant. This combination of great authentic food and Keralan culture and hospitality is summed up in Kayal's slogan – 'Where tradition meets quality'.

Kayal's founder Jaimon Thomas said it didn't take long for British diners to catch on. "From the day we opened people saw the difference in us. They came in with interest and maybe sometimes a little caution, but they went out with a smile and word quickly went around."

Kerala is a coastal, tropical land with a great abundance of fine seafood and vegetables. It's also a diverse place where Christian, Hindu and Muslim communities all contribute towards an exciting cuisine. There are biriyanis from the Mughlai tradition, dosas and vegetarian dishes from the Hindu communities and Christian dishes that show the complex historical interaction with European food, especially from Portuguese sailors.

So dishes such as Kayal fish curry made with king fish and a spicy coconut sauce reflects the maritime tradition, while Kumarakom duck roast is the traditional Easter celebration for Kerala's Syriac Christian community.

"We pick the best from all these traditions," says Jaimon. "There's a lot of history and character behind our food."

It's not just local diners who have taken to Kayal. People will often come to Leicester from all over England to try out Keralan food before they visit India. They often come again when they get back.

"It means a lot to us when that happens," says Jaimon. "It goes beyond just business – it's a source of real satisfaction to the team."

Leading national newspaper critics have found their way here too – a review by Matthew Norman described Kayal as "majestic ... this food genuinely is superb." Also celebrity chefs such as the Hairy Bikers, Paul Hollywood and Ainsley Harriot with Len Goodman have visited with film crews to learn some of the secrets of Kayal's chefs.

"We like to think we've helped focus attention on Leicester," adds Jaimon. "We're so pleased to be able to make our contribution to the city."

Kayal
BIJOCHAYAN'S CHEMMEEN KOOTU

Kayal's take on a Keralan seafood classic – use the biggest and best prawns
you can find! Serves 1.

Ingredients

2 tbsp oil

½ tsp mustard seeds

75g onion, finely chopped or minced

2 tomatoes, finely chopped

2 green chillies, chopped in half

1 tsp ginger, minced

½ tsp garlic, minced

2 strings curry leaves

1 tsp turmeric

1 tbsp coriander powder

25g coconut paste

50ml coconut milk

1 drumstick (an Indian vegetable
also know as moringa), chopped into
5cm pieces

5 large prawns, peeled

Salt to taste

To garnish

1 slice of tomato

Slices of mixed peppers (capsicum)

Curry leaves

Method

Heat the oil in a pan and fry the mustard seeds until they splutter. Add the onion, ginger, garlic, green chilli and most of the curry leaves and sauté until the onions are clear.

Add turmeric powder and coriander powder, sauté for a few more minutes. Add the tomatoes and coconut milk and sauté until the gravy becomes a semi-thick sauce.

Add the prawns and drumstick. Cover and allow it to cook – once the prawns are almost cooked, add coconut paste and salt to taste. Allow a few minutes until the prawns are fully cooked.

Remove from the heat, garnish with curry leaves, tomato and mix a capsicum.

You are ready!

RAMA DOSA

Dosas are especially popular throughout South India – this one uses added onions and chilli in the batter. Serves 1.

Ingredients

150g whole green gram (also known as mung beans)

2 tsp rice

75g onion, finely chopped

1 tsp cumin seeds

4 green chillies, minced

Salt to taste

Oil

Finely chopped onions for the topping

Method

Soak the green gram and rice together for 5-6 hours. Grind it to a smooth paste along with the onion, green chillies and salt until you have a batter. Add cumin seeds and mix well.

Heat a thava (a flat griddle pan), and pour a ladle of batter in the centre and spread it in a circular motion from the centre to the outside of the thava. Drizzle a teaspoon of oil around the dosa.

Sprinkle chopped onions on the top and press it lightly with a ladle or spatula.

When one side is done, flip it over to the other side, drizzle a little oil and cook until done.

Serve it with sambar (mixed vegetables in lentil sauce) and coconut chutney.

Life at THE MARKET

Exciting new developments are keeping Leicester's remarkable 700-year-old market at the very heart of city life.

Leicester Market really is one of the places that make the city so special. Not only is it Europe's biggest covered outdoor market, but in 2015 the new food hall was named Britain's Best Food Market.

At its core is a vibrant outdoor fruit and vegetable market. Open six days a week, it's a wonderful place – a proper, traditional market full of life and character where traders shout and vie for custom from the crowds, who in turn keep a sharp eye out for a bargain.

"You'll get the best prices on fruit and veg in the whole of Leicester," says Adam Piotrowski, development officer at the market. "There's a lot of on-site competition – if you're buying, say, strawberries, you can look around for whoever you think has the best deal on show."

The market also increasingly reflects Leicester's diversity with specialist stalls offering Indian and African Caribbean produce – everything from chillies, spices, gourds and okra to exotic fruit such as lychees, plantains and dragon fruit.

There's also that vastly improved indoor food hall. Gone is the dark, seventies building and now there is a modern, bright, better equipped space that has won numerous awards for its architecture and food offering. It's also helped bring in a younger generation of customers. "It's more appealing in just about every way," says Adam. "The feedback has been really positive, while the traders have upped their game and are enjoying the new space."

Inside there are eight traders – three butchers, two fishmongers and three deli-style stalls. It's the place to pick up fine cheeses from Leicestershire and beyond, a Melton Mowbray pork pie, top quality artisan bread, venison from Bradgate Park and great value, great quality beef, pork and lamb. The fishmongers are famous for the wide variety of fish from everyday cod, hake and plaice to outstanding turbot and halibut, along with shark, squid and the more unusual varieties that make them popular with the diverse communities of Leicester.

There are also three visiting continental markets a year on Gallowtree Gate and a Farmers Market on the first Thursday of the month. These regular markets make both top quality local produce and a wide range of European specialities available to the Leicester public.

Then there are special events such as the two massively popular food festivals held in the summer and winter. These attract some 20,000 customers along on a Sunday to visit more than 100 traders offering street food, local artisan produce and more. They are not only fun events for food enthusiasts but can be a launch pad for new cooks and food producers to test reaction to their produce.

"We're always looking for new traders who can offer something different and we try to support them with different levels at which they can start trading and progress."

Anyone looking for evidence of the Leicester Market effect need only look at Dunelm, the giant home furnishings store which started as a stall here in 1979. The company has not forgotten its roots or the great training in trading available and in 2016 held an apprentice-style event where applicants to their Leadership Programme had to run fruit, vegetable and flower stalls for the day.

The market website is a great source of information on what's happening and ideas for using the fine produce on sale. "We're selling fresh food and we want people to know what to do with it," said Adam. "So we've linked up with a local food blogger who loves the market and supplies us with recipes. He can respond quickly to what's available too. We also put on cooking demonstrations and have linked up with top local chefs to develop recipes using the best of local produce."

The pace of change at this ancient chartered market is relentless. As well as the creation of the new food hall, the last four years have seen new retail lock-ups, new management offices and new public toilets. There's also now two hot-food units on the outside of the food hall that offer a great opportunity for street food traders and others looking to develop their presence after the food festivals.

That's not the end of the improvements though. The market is part way through a multi-million pound programme that will also see the creation of a brand new public square where the old indoor market once stood. The space will help link up the old part of Leicester, now booming with the impact of the incredible events surrounding King Richard III, with the market and the rest of the city centre.

This much-loved part of Leicester life is surely set to thrive. "We're bringing all the market up to meet the level of our new food hall," said Adam. "There's so much potential here – we're really excited."

Leicester Market

Great
LITTLE BRITAIN

Bucking the trend of village pub closures by re-investing in classic British pubs.

Many pubs may have closed in recent years, but you will also hear industry insiders say that really great, well-run pubs never close.

This thought has fuelled the approach of the Leicestershire based Little Britain Pub Company. Since 2009 this family-run business has taken four somewhat tired and unloved village pubs and turned them around with a decent level of investment and a fresh food offering that has seen the drinkers and diners flock back.

The business was formed by two families – Mike and Lesley Herington and Ben and Katie Moore – with a background in pubs, design and property. The four used to go out in Woodhouse Eaves, and even as the economy tanked in 2009 they felt that they could make a difference to an under-used, investment-starved pub in that village, The Curzon Arms.

Their success led two years later to the purchase of The Windmill in Wymeswold and subsequently The Blue Bell in Rothley and The Crown in Old Dalby. Each time they've aimed to bring a bit of independent flair and restore the elements of what makes English pubs great – interesting design, real ales, roaring fires in winter, great outdoor spaces in summer, a thoughtful wine list and something exciting from the kitchen.

"The pubs share an ethos, but they're all distinctive to their village," says Mike. "The menus are all different and they change monthly so we can adapt to local demand. We are lucky to have fantastic staff, some of whom have been with us from the very start, they are crucial to the well-being of the pubs."

Where they can find the quality, the chefs look for local suppliers, for example The Windmill uses a butcher in nearby Syston, bread from Hambleton Bakery and cheese from Melton. Local breweries also feature, with Charnwood, Langton and Wicked Hathern often on show.

They are not resting on their laurels. "People are becoming more adventurous and the competition is stronger, our pubs will need to reflect this," says Mike. "There's a lot going on in Leicestershire – it's got a really good feel about it – we've recently purchased The Langton Arms in Church Langton to the south of Leicester where we will look to attract people from across that part of the county."

"Our basic aim is to do really good pub food," he concludes. "Not too clever, not too basic - the kind of place where you can enjoy a treat like our Chateaubriand, or turn up in jeans for a really good pie - it's that simple."

Little Britain Pub Co.

RARE ROAST CHATEAUBRIAND

A signature dish at The Windmill - this large steak is cut from the thickest part of the fillet and is bound to impress. For 2-3 to share.

Ingredients

For the Chateaubriand

450-500g Chateaubriand

20g fresh thyme

Cornish sea salt & pepper

25ml cold press rapeseed oil

50g butter

For the roast potatoes

750g medium maris piper potatoes, peeled

150g lard melted

10g celery salt

5g Cornish sea salt

5g cracked black pepper

Whole garlic bulb, cut in half

2 sprigs of thyme

For the heritage carrots

4 medium heritage carrots, peeled

50g butter

3g ground caraway seeds

300ml orange juice

50g caster sugar

For the horseradish sauce

5g fresh horseradish grated (add more if you want)

15g butter

300ml double cream

50ml white wine

Method

For the Chateaubriand

Pre-heat the oven at 200ºc

Remove the Chateaubriand from the fridge at least 20 minutes before cooking and season with salt and pepper.

Using a cast iron frying pan (one you can put in the oven) add rapeseed oil, heat until hot, add the Chateaubriand and seal all sides until golden brown, then add the butter and thyme.

Put in the oven for 15-20 minutes for rare.

Remove and rest for 10-15 minutes on a warm plate, cooking juices poured over, then cover with a clean tea towel.

For the horseradish sauce, bring the cream and wine to a boil and reduce by half. Add the fresh horseradish and butter and whisk until butter has melted.

For the roast potatoes

Pre-heat oven to 200ºc

Place potatoes in a pan, cover with water, add sea salt and boil until ¾ cooked, then drain and toss so the potatoes are ruffled. Put the potatoes in a heavy based roasting tin, sprinkle with celery salt, pepper, add garlic, thyme and lard.

Roast for 30-40 minutes until crispy on the outside

For the carrots

Add caraway seeds and butter to a pan, heat until the butter has melted. Add carrots, sugar, orange juice and water to cover the carrots.

Bring to the boil, cook until tender and the liquid is reduced to a syrup consistency.

To serve

Slice the Chateaubriand in to 4 slices, place potatoes and carrots on a large board. Place Chateaubriand on top of the carrots and sauce in a jug.

Gravy and Yorkies optional but definitely worthwhile!

OPEN FOR LUNCH
AND DINNER
7 DAYS A WEEK

Marquess of Exeter

PAN FRIED FILLET OF RED SNAPPER WITH ROASTED RED PEPPER, SPRING ONION & GINGER SALSA

Simple, fresh, delicious. Serves 4.

The Marquess of Exeter in Lyddington is a handsome pub in possibly Rutland's most handsome village. It's exceptional for its dreamy, honey-hued ironstone buildings, and there's also an exceptional hand guiding the kitchen.
Chef Brian Baker is a local lad who started his career as a butcher's boy in Uppingham. But he went on to become the youngest chef to ever hold a Michelin star during his time at Hambleton Hall, and then a stellar career taking in spells as private chef to Elton John and the designer Valentino, and running both top London restaurants and massive banqueting operations.
The draw home to a simpler life eventually proved too strong and the Marquess proved the ideal venue to run a pub with great food that stayed approachable.
It's no identikit gastropub but a destination restaurant that still manages to be a hub for the local community.

Ingredients

4 red snapper fillets (150-180g each)

Selection of baby leaves

Salt & pepper

Olive oil

For the salsa

3 red peppers, roasted, skinned, de-seeded and chopped

4 spring onions, finely chopped

2½cm fresh ginger, grated

Half bunch fresh coriander, finely chopped

Half bunch fresh mint, finely chopped

Juice of 2 limes

150ml rapeseed oil

Method

Season the fish. Heat the olive oil in a pan and add the fillets skin side down. Fry on each side for 3-4 minutes, then leave to rest in a warm place.

Mix all the salsa ingredients together and season.

To assemble, arrange the mixed baby leaves in the middle of the plate and top with the fish. Add a spoonful of salsa onto the fish and drizzle with olive oil.

The PIE MINISTER

Leicestershire and Rutland has an extraordinary food heritage – and Matthew O'Callaghan has been vital to celebrating and extending it.

In the mid 1990s parts of rural Leicestershire were struggling, with BSE ("Mad Cow disease") having knocked confidence in British produce.

Some 20 years later the area is England's "Capital of Rural Food", playing host to numerous prestige food festivals, fairs and events and attracting some £70 million of food tourism every year.

What on earth changed? The man to ask is one of Leicestershire's genuine food heroes - Matthew O'Callaghan OBE.

Newly-elected as a Melton Borough councillor, Matthew saw an opportunity to exploit Leicestershire's wonderful food heritage and called a meeting that would lead to the Melton Mowbray Food Partnership.

He also needed a good campaign. And that came when he saw a Marks and Spencer pork pie that was heavily branded as a Melton Mowbray pie but had pink, cured meat so it was nothing of the sort! An attempted prosecution under trading standards failed, but that just prompted the indefatigable O'Callaghan to lead an 11 year campaign through the courts until the mighty Melton pork pie was eventually given Protected Food Name status by the European Union.

As a result not only are consumers across the world assured of a better pie, but new producers have opened up locally and can be assured of getting a good price for this premium product.

"But there's been a wider agenda too," says Matthew. "We've established the Melton Food Festival, we set up one of the first Farmer's Markets, and we've kept our cattle market in the town centre and invested in it."

The wonderfully atmospheric cattle market, which also hosts collectibles fairs and fur and feather markets is a town jewel and another important element in bringing tourism.

Matthew has also helped establish the British Pie Awards and the Artisan Cheese Fair, the largest cheese fair in the country which features some 300 cheeses. "We've got Stilton the king of cheeses, but we've also got Red Leicester, Colwick, Slipcote - so we should be the capital of cheese," says Matthew. Other events to follow include PieFest and ChocFest.

There's a great history of food in Leicestershire and Rutland – from the first ever wedding cake recipe by the Countess of Rutland in the 17th century to the pioneering work of Robert Bakewell in breeding cattle.

"Yes, we've got great heritage but we are trend setters too," emphasises Matthew. "The range of ethnic food, especially in Leicester is unique and we've got rural businesses producing paneer, Japanese tofu and halal lamb. It's amazing what we've got here."

Matthew O'Callaghan
MELTON EMPANADAS

These pasties are originally from Chile, but this is my local (vegetarian) version of them. I've also included the meat option. Makes 6-8 empanadas.

Ingredients

For the pastry

500g sifted plain flour from Whissendine Mill

150g vegetable shortening (lard for the meat version) at room temperature

Pinch of salt

200ml warm water, approximately

For the filling

250g vegetarian mince or Quorn (or minced beef)

2 large onions

2 hard-boiled eggs

½ tsp paprika

1 tsp ground cumin

Salt and pepper to taste

50g raisins

Olives are in the traditional recipe but I don't like these so I don't include them

Method

To prepare the pastry, add salt to flour and lightly rub in fat. Slowly add the water until an elastic dough is obtained. Knead the dough lightly. Store in the fridge for 30 minutes.

For the filling, fry the onion until golden in vegetable oil (or lard for meat version). Add the mince which should be moist (use vegetable stock if needed for vegetarian mince), add cumin, paprika, pepper and salt and continue until fully integrated. Allow to cool.

Roll out the pastry into circles around the size of a tea plate (17cm) and moisten the edges with water. Put a few spoons of filling into each – don't over fill. Now add raisins, a quarter boiled egg and, if desired, olives.

Seal and crimp the pasty. For a nice finish, glaze with egg yolk or milk. Put on a baking tray in the middle of a pre-heated oven at 200ºc. Bake until golden brown (around 15 minutes).

The real
FARMER'S MARKET

A busy market offering great quality, great value and the warmest of welcomes.

There has been a market in Melton Mowbray for 1,000 years and it is recorded in the Domesday Book. What is unique about Melton's Farmers' Market is that it sits alongside the largest remaining town centre livestock market in the country. This makes it a truly farm to fork experience, with butchers buying stock from the livestock market to sell to customers in the farmers market.

"Good value and top quality – that's what we offer," says market organiser Lin Machin. "It's also an incredibly friendly place – the traders are all happy to have a laugh and it's the warm welcome that keeps people coming back."

The Farmers' Market takes place every Tuesday, Friday and the first Saturday of the month offering a range of fresh fruit and vegetables, meat, fish, cheese, speciality foods and crafts. There is a weekly "Fur and Feather" market selling live poultry, ducks, rabbit as well as a game auction in season. It's great theatre and offers an authentic slice of real food and real farming.

"From butcher to fishmonger to cheese and samosas – we're here for the community" says Lin.

We asked some of the regular traders to pen a few words about their business:

Cook's Kitchen

Cook's Kitchen uses quality ingredients and free-range eggs, to make a wide variety of cakes (including gluten and dairy free), pastries and scones. There's also Fairtrade tea and coffee – not just a market unit, but a little tea-room.

Ownsworth's

Ownsworth's Rapeseed Oil is grown, pressed and bottled on our family farm and vineyard. Cold pressed, simply filtered and fully traceable. There are no chemicals added to hinder the natural taste of our high quality oil. It is rich in vitamins, with half the saturated fat of olive oil. Perfect for roasting, frying and barbecuing.

Cards by Marilyn

Unique handmade cards for all occasions. Special orders by request.

Fair Game Foods

Fair Game Foods invite you to come and try their famous succulent pork roast rolls. Professional, quality outside catering, with over 15 years' experience, they seek to promote locally sourced ingredients.

Slightly Potty

Slightly Potty offers every aspect of silk flowers – from loose flowers to a special occasion arrangement. They were awarded a Royal Warrant in 2009 by the Queen, and have provided silk flowers for most of the royal residences.

19 Gales

19 Gales Farmhouse Foods is a family business run by third generation farmers. The farm has a mixture of grass for grazing and cereals to feed their outdoor herd of British Blue cattle. This is food grown by farmers, made by farmers, sold by farmers.

Old Brickyard Garden Tea

Discover the fascinating world of tea with Anna Stasinska of the Old Brickyard Tea Garden. Anna, aka Tea Lady, has travelled widely from Darjeeling to Japan, and loves to share her tea experiences. She offers tastings and talks at her tearoom and elsewhere.

Scarborough Fayre

Scarborough Fayre has been trading for 18 years, selling top quality fresh fish, shellfish and game. They pride themselves on the products that they supply to both retail and catering customers.

Hambleton Bakery

In September 2008, Julian Carter and Tim Hart opened Hambleton Bakery to produce top quality, traditionally made bread. The bakery now has retail outlets in Exton, Oakham, Market Harborough, West Bridgford, Melton Mowbray and Stamford.

Grasmere Farm

At Grasmere Farm they are passionate about providing affordable, delicious food that is hand crafted by our butchers and cooks. We combine the benefits of old fashioned farming methods and a blend of innovative yet traditional recipes. Grasmere Farm is proud of its reputation for sausages, from traditional Lincolnshire to the unique flavour of smoked Rutland sausage.

Handmade Alice

They design and make everything from bags, purses and wallets to cushions, wall art and decorations, along with a clothing alteration service. They make gifts and accessories that are colourful, cheerful and functional. Their style is a pic'n'mix of vintage, rock, romantic, cute and a good dose of humour!

Robert Bowring Farmer and Butchers

Established over 30 years ago supplying quality British meat, all their beef is born, reared and fattened on their East Midlands family farm.

Since starting at Melton Mowbray they have built a regular customer base with customers coming from all over the country to the famous Tuesday market. They're proud to have won numerous gold awards for our pies and sausages.

The Market Tavern

Di and her team offer a warm welcome to the many customers who return time and again to enjoy their locally sourced produce whether for a Full English or the popular pie at lunchtime, enjoyed with a pint or a tea/coffee.

Schedule

Tuesdays - Weekly livestock, Fur and Feather, Farmers Market, Antiques and General Market

Fridays - Farmers and Antiques Market

1st Saturday of the month - Farmers Market, Horse Sale

Check website for more details and special events - www.meltonmowbraymarket.co.uk

Melton Mowbray Market

The perfect
VILLAGE PUB

A fast-growing, family-run food and drink business in the heart of Charnwood.

"I think we're at the start of something quite special," enthuses Jay Cooledge. "We're brimming over with ideas and enthusiasm. With Odd John we're building a platform to turn great ideas into reality."

The eponymous Odd John is Jay's dad - a lovable, eccentric character who from 2001 ran the Griffin Inn in the beautiful Charnwood village of Swithland. Jay worked for his dad for nearly a decade before getting more involved in the business in 2010.

The pub itself has been smartened up and quietly evolved into a welcoming, unpretentious "real food" pub that avoids gastropub territory. Its menu of classics, local and seasonal specials such as Bradgate Park venison pie has a big appeal to locals, walkers, cyclists, horse-riders and everyone else.

Then the rather damp old skittle alley out the back has been turned into the light and beautiful Old Stables, now one of the top wedding venues in the county, celebrating around 100 nuptials every year.

In 2015 came Odd John's Kitchen, a quirky, homely, country-kitchen cafe and deli across the yard. With soup bubbling away on the Aga its like popping round to your Mum's for tea. It's only small but there's a range of chutneys, jams, teas and coffee, plus a few cheeses and meats and a range of delicious snacks prepared by another new Odd John initiative – a craft bakery set up in Hamilton that supplies artisan bread for the pub along with cakes, biscuits and delicious sweet and savoury pastries.

There will be plenty to keep the bakery busy as Odd John's has also now taken on the Falcon Inn in Long Whatton and in late Spring 2016 will be opening a full-size Odd John's deli in the heart of nearby Quorn. They have gone the crowdfunding route, so as to give the community a chance to get involved in the business.

Behind it all, giving sage advice to balance Jay's youthful enthusiasm, lies the figure of Odd John himself, now immortalised in the company logo enjoying a quiet pint, with a background visual echo of the famous Old John landmark in Bradgate. It seems entirely right for an innovative, entrepreneurial company that remains rooted in family values.

Odd John & Family Ltd

Odd John's
PORK PIE

Our take on the local speciality 'pork pie'. Made with a pork and tarragon terrine, and apple jelly, and a shortcrust pastry rectangle. It is flavoured with a Charnwood-made Burleighs gin for good measure!

Ingredients

1kg pork shoulder

568ml apple juice

2 large banana shallots

6 gelatine leaves

35g tarragon

70ml Burleighs London Dry Gin

2 tsp Dijon mustard

1.1 litres chicken stock

50g butter

Salt and pepper

Ready to roll puff pastry

Method

Rub the pork shoulder with the salt and mustard. Fill a large roasting tin with the chicken stock and submerge the pork. Foil the tin and place in a pre-heated oven at 160ºc for about 3 hours, or until tender throughout. Meanwhile dice and sweat the shallots in a frying pan with the butter, set aside. Once the pork is cooked remove carefully from the stock and allow to cool slightly.

Strip the pork, breaking it up between fingers until you achieve a pulled pork-type texture. Add the shallots and tarragon leaves, roughly chopped and mix through the pork.

Line a terrine mould with two layers of cling film pushing well into the corners. Add the pork mixture to the terrine mould and fold excess cling film over to cover the top of the pork, pressing down with hand. Place another terrine mould on top of the pork and apply weight (a couple of tins of beans should do the trick). Place the terrine in the fridge for 2-3 hours or until completely cooled and set.

For the jelly, heat the apple juice in a pan but do not allow to boil. Meanwhile, soak the gelatine leaves in cold water until soft and squeeze out excess water. Remove the apple juice from stove and add the gin and softened gelatine. Stir well. Cover a flat tray that has raised sides with cling film and pour in the mixture and place in fridge for 1-2 hours until the jelly has set.

When ready to serve, remove weight from the top of the terrine and turn out onto a chopping board and slice. Turn out the jelly on to a chopping board and slice into the desired shape. Cut the pastry into a rectangle and bake until golden. Allow the terrine to come back up to room temperature before serving.

Odd John's
DUO OF BRADGATE VENISON

Tasty local meat cooked two ways with a fine local beer.

Ingredients

600g Bradgate Park venison leg, diced

220g Bradgate venison loin

½ medium onion, diced to 5mm

1 clove garlic, diced to 5mm

2 carrots, large dice, diced to 10mm

3 sprigs fresh thyme

1 bay leaf

5g plain flour

200g wild mushrooms, roughly chopped

100g butter

100ml cold pressed rapeseed oil

1 egg

1 sheet ready to roll puff pastry

500ml Old School Beer – Charnwood Brewery

Method

Firstly, 'test' 200ml of the Charnwood Brewery Old School, y'know, just to make sure it's okay!

Place large saucepan over a medium heat and melt the butter in the pan. Add the diced onion, sweat until almost soft, add garlic and sweat for further two minutes. Add mushrooms and thyme leaves and fry for 3 minutes then take off heat. Coat the diced venison in seasoned flour. Heat up a little oil in a heavy bottomed, oven proof pan on a high heat and add the venison. Put the mushroom and onion mix into the pan with the venison, add the bay leaf. Gradually add the ale, stirring constantly to avoid lumps, season to taste. Pour into a casserole dish, cover and place in oven at 160ºc until tender.

For the pastry lid, cut around the casserole dish leaving a 1cm border. Beat the egg and coat the pastry using a pastry brush. Allow to dry and repeat to give the pastry a better colour and shine.

After the mix is tender, pull out and remove cover. Place the pastry lid over the top, crimp edges but do not seal. Pierce the centre of the pastry and put back into the oven to cook until golden.

Sear the venison loin in a smoking hot pan, turning until caramelised all around and place in oven and cook to liking. Best served rare. Allow to rest for 2-3 minutes before carving.

A good way to serve might be with fondant potatoes and purple sprouting broccoli.

SIMON'S LITTLE TART

Using ready made pastry makes this a delightfully simple, light lemon tart.

350g of unsalted butter (1cm cubes)

8 whole eggs

4 yolks

6 lemons, juice and zest

300g caster sugar

1 sheet ready rolled sweet shortcrust pastry

Grease tartlet tins with butter, dust with flour and push pastry into tartlet tins, line with parchment and fill with rice/baking beans. Blind bake until cooked at 180ºc (around 12 mins). Allow to cool and shave off excess pastry.

Beat the eggs, yolks, sugar, zest and juice in a mixing bowl over simmering water until the mixture starts to emulsify and add the butter. Whisk further until butter is melted and pour into the pastry cases. Refrigerate to set.

Classic dishes
WITH A TWIST

Lively village dining pub offering a home from home whatever the time of year.

The Old Bull's Head has been a pub since the 19th century and has long been a key hub for the lovely village of Woodhouse Eaves. But over the last decade it has established itself as a big, busy dining pub serving classics with a twist.

Located within the spectacular hills of Charnwood Forest it serves a wide-ranging clientele from walkers, to village regulars and people coming out from the city for special events. Being only 10 minutes off the M1 it attracts long-distance travellers too.

Inside this lovely old building you'll find a modern, clean and crisp interior that still upholds a bit of rustic charm. It's a pub that manages to change with the seasons from a being a place for sitting by the fire with newspapers in winter to enjoying al fresco dining in the summer. It's also famous for its impressive glass-walled wine cellar in the centre of the restaurant that regularly acts as a talking point or photo opportunity for diners. As well as crowd-pleasing zesty sauvignon blancs and aromatic riojas, you can find fine wines tucked away in there, including Chassagne Montrachet, Barolo and Dom Pérignon champagne.

"The menu has two main styles" explains deputy manager Jade Fletcher, one luxurious and indulgent, one with a focus on the light and healthy.

"If you are pushing the boat out, there might be a Chateaubriand steak to share and different options with lobster and prawns," she explains. "But you will also find dishes such as chicken, bacon and avocado salad which is really light and fresh."

The pub is proud of its place in the local community and has adopted the James McCarthy Foundation as its charity, including directing some of the proceeds from this book. The charity raises awareness about undiagnosed brain tumours, including training more doctors to spot the symptoms early on. "We just want to do anything we can to help," says Jade.

"This pub is a dream to manage," she continues. "We've got a really diverse but close knit team here who are intent on personalising everyone's experience. We see great service and quality going hand in hand. We think of everyone as a guest not a customer – it's like we're inviting them into our home, a place of which we're very proud."

Old Bull's Head

VENISON STEAK WITH FONDANT POTATO AND CHOCOLATE JUS

Serves 2

Ingredients

100g tenderstem broccoli

2 wedges of fresh pineapple

40ml chocolate sauce

100ml veal jus/beef stock

2 venison steaks

2 baking potatoes

60g butter

Pinch of thyme

Salt and pepper to season

Method

Peel the potatoes and shape into cubes. Melt the butter in a pan with thyme, salt and pepper. Add the potatoes, stirring and turning until areas are well covered.

Put the potatoes in an oven dish and fill with water until around half way up the potatoes. Cook for 20 minutes at 180ºc.

Cook the venison in a frying pan to your personal preference ensuring that all edges are sealed.

Put the pineapple on a tray in the oven. Boil or steam the broccoli until cooked. Add the chocolate sauce to the veal jus and stir well until fully combined.

Serve the venison on top of the broccoli, pineapple and fondant potato with chocolate jus over and around the dish.

Old Bull's Head

KING PRAWN, CHORIZO & CRAB LINGUINE

Serves 2

Ingredients

1 red chilli, chopped

100g fresh plum tomatoes

20g flat leaf parsley

20ml extra virgin olive oil

1 garlic bulb, finely chopped

100g chorizo sausage

80g crab claw meat

30ml sweet chilli sauce

160g peeled king prawns

200ml white wine

180g linguine

Lemon zest to garnish

Salt and pepper to taste

Method

Chop the tomatoes (around 1 cm dice), parsley, garlic and chilli and mix in a bowl with the sweet chilli sauce and olive oil.

In a hot, oiled pan, place the chorizo and prawns and cook until the prawns turn pink. Add the tomato mix, white wine and crab meat and bring to a simmer. Season to taste.

Cook the linguine in salted water with a dash of olive oil as per the packet cooking instructions.

Drain the pasta and add to the pan with the rest of the dish and stir to fully coat the linguine.

Serve in a pasta bowl with lemon zest over the top to garnish.

My family's
SECRET RECIPES

Popular Indian restaurant serving dishes with recipes passed down through the generations.

Tucked away in a former pub on a side road off Catherine Street, Paddy's Marten Inn was for a few years something of an underground success. But food this good was never going to be secret for long and now it's renowned as one of the busiest and best Indian restaurants in the region.

Established in 1996 this lively, unpretentious, hugely enjoyable restaurant is built on recipes passed down through generations of the Mashru family. With over 170 dishes on the menu there is huge choice from sizzling grills and traditional curries to vegetarian dishes served in the style of the simple roadside dhabas across India – the likes of gungo peas with methi and aubergine. Other popular dishes include the East African-influenced chicken machoosi, tangy lamb chop curry and fabulously fresh-tasting fish fillets topped with a green Gujarati masala. The popular Indo-Chinese style is represented too.

Paddy's draws in people from all over the city and from all of Leicester's diverse communities to experience both the exceptional food and the buzzing atmosphere. Sitting among pictures of old Bollywood stars, diners are served with enthusiasm and efficiency – it gets pretty lively but service levels never seem to waver.

Word has not just got out among Leicester diners but has reached the likes of Jamie Oliver too. In 2011 he visited Leicester to shop at Leicester market with owner and chef Amita Mashru who cooked alongside him in the kitchen for his programme Jamie Oliver's Great Britain.

Amita's son Raj Mashru explained his Mum still heads up the kitchen and makes sure the food going out is consistently excellent: "Our dishes come from our own secret family recipes, so you won't find food that tastes quite the same anywhere else," says Raj. "We are, and always will be, devoted to providing the finest traditional Indian food to the people of Leicester and visitors from further afield."

Paddy's Marten Inn

AMITA'S SLOW-COOKED LAMB ON THE BONE

Slow-cooking lamb this way helps the flavours to mature
and the meat to become really tender. Serves 4.

Ingredients

700g lamb on the bone, cut into small pieces

4 tbsp vegetable oil

4 bay leaves

5 green cardamom

2cm cinnamon stick

5 cloves

4 large onions, diced

3 tomatoes, chopped

1 tbsp ginger paste

2 tbsp garlic paste

2 tbsp green chilli paste

½ tsp turmeric

2 tsp coriander powder

1 tsp kasoori methi (dried fenugreek leaves)

Salt to taste

To garnish

Small handful chopped coriander

Method

Heat oil in a large pan.

Add the bay leaves, cardamom, cinnamon and cloves.

When the leaves begin to sizzle and release fragrance, add the onions and sauté until light golden brown, stirring frequently.

Stir in the ginger, garlic and green chilli paste.

Now add the lamb and season, adding a little water if necessary to avoid the lamb sticking to the pan. Simmer for 15 minutes.

Add turmeric, coriander powder and kasoori methi.

Now add 5 tablespoons of water and the chopped tomatoes, continuing to stir for 5 minutes.

Add more water to the level of the meat and reduce the heat.

Simmer slowly until the meat is tender and the sauce has thickened.

Garnish with fresh coriander and serve with basmati rice, naan bread, roti or chapati.

Paddy's Marten Inn
AMITA'S JINGA MASTI

This king prawn dish is a popular choice on the menu at Paddy's – here's a simple version you can try at home. Serves 1.

Ingredients

5 jumbo prawns in the shell, butterflied

1 tbsp olive oil

1 tsp ginger paste

1 tsp garlic paste

½ lemon

½ tsp garam masala

1 tsp coriander powder

1 tsp kasoori methi (dried fenugreek leaves)

½ onion, processed into a paste

1 tomato, finely diced

Salt to taste

To garnish

Fresh coriander leaves

Method

Heat the oil in a large pan, add the prawns and stir fry.

When the prawns begin to sizzle, add a pinch of salt.

Add the garlic and ginger paste and stir for 2 minutes.

Mix in the onion paste and diced tomatoes and continue stirring.

Add the coriander powder, garam masala and kasoori methi.

Squeeze in the juice of half a lemon and leave to simmer on a low heat until the sauce is thickened.

Add fresh coriander and serve.

All hail THE QUEEN

Independent spirit, fine beers and casual dining in the heart of Leicester.

The success of the Queen of Bradgate speaks volumes about the way Leicester's food and drink businesses are fighting back, and how the independent sector can find its place alongside the corporate world.

Owner Matt Saunders has owned and run some 30 pubs and bars since the early 1990s and wasn't necessarily looking for another. But he was aware that things were stirring on Leicester's High Street with the big restaurant chains falling over themselves to take space in and around Highcross.

The Queen of Bradgate had been empty for a while and had not always had the greatest reputation. "But it had a great shape, a great layout and the footfall was increasing," says Matt. "I wanted to do a craft beer bar, not replicate what had gone before. It took us six months to shake off that reputation but eventually we started to get traction."

It remains a drinks-led pub with eight hand-pulled real ales, a wide selection of craft beers and lagers and a sectioned off, bookable cocktail bar area that specialises in gin. But Matt also says he's tried to create "the kind of pub I'd like to eat in."

It's not fine dining – it's approachable, freshly prepared pub food that contains a few twists and surprises. Unpretentious but nicely conceived and presented dishes such as crispy ham hock and Gruyère fritters with English mustard mayonnaise have been much lauded by local food bloggers. The one dish that is undroppable is their take on chilli con carne, prepared with cubes of slow cooked shin of beef and served in a mess tin with home made nachos, guacamole and sour cream.

"We've got three brilliant chefs and we've invested £60,000 in the kitchen," says Matt. "Now food sales are up 60 per cent year on year, so I think we're gaining a reputation."

The pub already has live music nights but is also now developing its fabulous upstairs space into a dedicated music venue, which will also further improve the ambience for diners.

"I wanted to create my perfect boozer," says Matt. "Looking around, I think that's what we've done."

Queen of Bradgate
SHIN OF BEEF CHILLI

A constant on the Queen of Bradgate menu since it opened, this recipe uses a
slow cooker to take your usual chilli to another level. Serves 6.

Ingredients

1kg diced shin of beef

1 onion, diced

5 garlic cloves, crushed

2 chillies, chopped

50g coriander stalks, chopped

Handful of coriander leaves, chopped

1 cinnamon stick

2 tsp ground cumin

1 tsp ground coriander

1 tsp chilli powder

1 tsp caraway seeds

3 tbsp tomato purée

2 tins chopped tomatoes

1 tin kidney beans

425ml beef stock

Vegetable oil for frying

Salt and pepper to season

Method

Heat a little oil in a frying pan and add half the shin and brown evenly. Place the meat in a slow cooker and repeat with the remaining beef.

Return the pan to the heat and add a little more oil and then the onions, coriander stalks, chillies and garlic. Continue to fry on a low heat until soft for about 5 minutes. Add all the dry spices and fry until fragrant then place in to the slow cooker with the beef.

Return the pan to the heat and add the beef stock and carefully deglaze the pan.

Finally add the chopped tomatoes, tomato purée and the beef stock to the rest of the ingredients and stir well. Place the lid on the slow cooker and cook on a low heat for 7 hours until the meat begins to fall apart.

Add the kidney beans and cook for a further 30 minutes.

Season to taste and finish with a handful of coriander stirred through.

Destination DINING

A stylish North West Leicestershire inn with a growing reputation for great food.

When in 2010 Chris and Alex Astwood had the chance to take on the newly-refurbished Royal Oak, they didn't have to think twice.

The brothers had 20 years' of experience in the hospitality industry but were looking to move away from fine dining and towards doing great food in a village pub, preferably with hotel rooms.

The Royal Oak in Long Whatton was ideal for them to implement their ideas.

"We have a strong focus on using fresh produce to make really high quality pub food," says Chris. "We make pretty much everything ourselves. There are micro-herbs from our own garden and we get a lot of vegetables from locals – whenever things are in season our kitchen door is always open." Great East Midlands produce is featured across the menu, with local suppliers proudly listed.

The menu reflects the pub's diverse range of guests. "We have pub classics but everything is done to the absolute best of our ability," says Chris. "There are fish and chips, but it will have our own pea purée, hand cut triple-cooked chips and so on."

But young chef James Upton, who worked with the Astwoods on previous ventures, also shows the kind of flair that has won the kitchen an AA rosette and a Michelin guide listing, with ambitious dishes such as 'All Things Beef' featuring sous-vide fillet, braised short-rib sausage roll, oxtail and Guinness jus.

Drinkers are well catered for too, with local brewers Charnwood featured strongly – "The minute we tried their beer we knew we had to have it" says Chris – and 15 wines from the extensive list are available by the glass.

The pub is firmly rooted in its village but has also become a destination dining pub for this part of the East Midlands. Indeed its proximity to Donington race track, East Midlands Airport and the university town of Loughborough is helping it gain an international following. Business and leisure travellers staying in its AA four star gold award rooms are delighted to find high quality à la carte dining on site. The breakfasts have won awards too.

"We've a great manager who used to work with Gordon Ramsay and we really pride ourselves on our relaxed but efficient service," says Chris.

The pub looked an ideal match for the Astwoods' ambition, and that's just how it has turned out.

APPLE WOOD SMOKED CHICKEN BOURGUIGNON

A smokey take on the French classic. Home smoking needs care but it's worth the effort.

Ingredients

For the pine nut crumble

100g butter

50g caster sugar

100g plain flour

50g toasted pine nuts

For the pancetta crisps

8 slices of pancetta (thin cut)

For the potato spaghetti

2 medium peeled potatoes

2 tbsp vegetable oil

For the chicken

4 chicken supreme, skin on, bone in French trimmed

50g apple wood smoking chips

For the squash purée

1 butternut squash, peeled and diced into 1-2 cm cubes.

Sprig of thyme

250ml double cream

For the bourguignon garnish

20 chestnut mushrooms

20 silverskin onions or baby shallots

4 chopped garlic cloves

Knob of butter

Sprig of thyme

For the bourguignon sauce

250ml red wine

2 chopped garlic cloves

1 diced Spanish onion

100g pancetta, diced

Sprig of thyme

1 tbsp plain flour

200ml good quality beef stock

1 tbsp tomato purée

Method

The pine nut crumble, pancetta crisps and potato spaghetti can be done in advance.

For the pine nut crumble

Crush half the nuts and mix the flour, sugar and butter. Put all of the ingredients, onto a baking tray and cook at 160°c for 8-10 minutes, turning occasionally.

For the pancetta crisps

Lay the pancetta slices on a greaseproof baking tray, add another layer of greaseproof paper and sandwich with another baking tray. Cook at 120°c for an hour, or until the pancetta is golden.

For the potato spaghetti

Use a spiraliser on the potatoes to make the spaghetti. In a bowl mix the potato and oil and add seasoning. Wrap greaseproof paper around the outside of a metal ring mould or metal pastry cutter then wrap the spaghetti around the outside of the metal mould. Place the ring on a baking tray in the oven at 120°c for 20 minutes.

In a 140°c preheated fryer add the potato complete with greaseproof ring for 3-4 minutes until golden. Allow to cool slightly, before slipping the potato off the metal ring.

For the chicken

Add the smoke chips to a baking tray, on top place a wire rack with the chicken on. Cover with a lid or foil and cook on the hob on low for 8 minutes. Add the olive oil to a hot frying pan, then the chicken skin side down for 2 minutes. Transfer to a baking tray and cook in the oven at 180°c for 10-12 minutes until cooked through.

For the purée

Put the butternut squash, cream and thyme in a saucepan. Cook on a medium heat for 15-20 minutes until the butternut squash is soft. Season to taste and blend the mixture.

For the bourguignon garnish

On a medium heat add the olive oil to a pan and cook the mushrooms and onions for 3 minutes. Reduce the heat to low and add the garlic, thyme, butter and seasoning. Cook for 5-7 minutes or until soft and tender.

For the bourguignon sauce

Fry the pancetta on a medium heat for 4-5 minutes. Add the chopped onion, garlic, flour, tomato purée and thyme. Add red wine and cook until the wine reduces by half and then add the beef stock. Cook for 5 minutes.

To serve

Create a smear of purée, and add the potato ring so that it sits on top. Dot the mushroom and onion garnish around the plate and add the sliced chicken. Add the pancetta and sauce and spinkle on the crumble.

Riding the
CREST OF A WAVE

Premium British charcuterie made on a Rutland farm
is making a big name for itself.

Many English people dream of living in France. Few of them get to do it. Fewer still do it, come back and start a successful business making fine Mediterranean-inspired charcuterie.

That, though, is the story of former cabinet maker Nick Brake. Rutland Charcuterie is now leading a new wave of artisan food makers that are revolutionising charcuterie by showing that Brits can do as well as if not better than anyone.

"We've got the best livestock in the world, there's no reason we can't make the best charcuterie," insists Nick.

There is a great tradition of curing and smoking in the UK but our climate has not been ideal for the air-dried meats of the Mediterranean nations. Now though there is the technology for climate control that means Nick can now make the likes of his stunning Coppa, an air-dried meat made from the neck muscle of the pig which delivers huge depth of flavour.

Then there's the succulent Bresaola made from Leicestershire beef, wafer thin slices of delicious Noix de Jambon, the classic fennel salami along with their award-winning garlic salami.

The business started after Nick and his family returned from living and working in the French Alps and he completed a year-long diploma course in charcuterie at the School of Artisan Food in Nottinghamshire. He passed with distinction and with the contacts he had made, he was ready to go.

There's been considerable local support to this exciting new business and the "Made in Rutland" tag is of tremendous marketing value. Nick has coined the Rutland motto – "Multum in Parvo" or "Much in Little" - which perfectly sums up the air-drying process which intensifies the taste, the flavour and the colour of these amazing charcuterie products made from simple quality ingredients.

Since winning a coveted place on the Grocery Accelerator scheme, business has boomed and the message about using free range meat to produce premium local products, made with an absolute regard for animal welfare, is clearly getting across.

There is a growing demand for the highest quality British charcuterie from discerning retailers and consumers. "British charcuterie is gaining momentum and we're happy to be riding the crest of a wave," says Nick "We really want to continue to build on the success of British charcuterie and I'm looking forward to the day when we can start exporting it back into the Mediterranean!"

Rutland Charcuterie Co.
ROASTED VEGETABLE AND CHARCUTERIE BOARD

The ingredients can all be prepared in advance – it then takes minutes to assemble. For best results use a griddle pan to char the vegetables. The charred stripes from the griddle pan really stand out against the other ingredients. We present this on a long oak table board made by a local company Bradgate Woodcraft in the heart of the Charnwood Forest. This certainly helps in making this a very impressive dish. A starter for 10!

Ingredients

1 large aubergine, thinly sliced lengthways

2 courgettes, thinly sliced lengthways

3 red peppers, cut into quarters lengthways with stalks attached

70g wild rocket

125g pesto

250g mozzarella, torn into bite size pieces

50g caper berries

50g black olives

700g air-dried meats, thinly sliced (e.g. coppa, duck prosciutto, bresaola)

Lemon juice, to drizzle

Olive oil, to drizzle

Balsamic vinegar, to drizzle

Black Pepper

Method

To prepare the vegetables

Pre-heat oven to 240ºc.

Salt the aubergine in a bowl for 20 minutes.

Drizzle the peppers with olive oil and roast for 20 minutes.

Wash off the aubergine and thoroughly pat dry, then drizzle with olive oil.

Griddle the aubergine and courgette slices on both sides until soft.

Drizzle the courgette with olive oil and lemon juice.

To assemble

Put the wild rocket down the centre of the presentation board and then drizzle with olive oil and balsamic vinegar.

Put groups of the roasted peppers at intervals down the board and fill with a teaspoon of pesto. Arrange all the other ingredients along the board, arranging the air-dried meats in batches.

Season with a crack of black pepper.

You could use any number of different ingredients – sliced salami, artichoke hearts, sun-dried tomatoes and roasted asparagus for example would all work well.

Sloe-ly SPIRITED

Celebrating the English countryside with spirits made from fruits and hedgerow berries using traditional methods.

Imagine a bright crisp, November morning on a Rutland hillside. Amid the mists and mellow fruitfulness, something stirs in the hedgerow. Is it a deer? No, hang on, it's Andy Hoyle, and he's hard at work collecting blue-black jewels from the blackthorn bushes.

For Andy is the man behind Sloeberry Spirits, a definitive rural microbusiness run out of a barn at the celebrated Northfield Farm north of Oakham producing a small but compelling range of English berry fruit spirits. And key to the Melton Mowbray-branded selection is their award-winning sloe gin.

Like many of us, it was his granny who had first introduced Andy to this countryside tradition. Years later in 2010 when he was looking for a new opportunity in life, the chance to take over this small but well-regarded business came along and he grabbed it.

Now he produces some 4,000 bottles a year, around a third of which are the crystal-clear, purple nectar granny made so well. She would absolutely recognise the techniques he uses – it's just fruit, gin (a traditional London dry) and sugar. There's no automation here – in fact one of the few innovations Andy has introduced is using large pans for the maceration. Well have you ever tried pushing 500kg of fruit through the neck of a demi-john?

Along with the sloe gin, the company produces a raspberry gin, blackberry vodka, strawberry vodka and whisky and wild damson.

"Almost everyone who tries that loves it," says Andy with a grin. "Even those who insist they don't like whisky."

During the summer months Andy and his family can be found out and about promoting their produce at food fairs and festivals, but you can also find the elegant, evocative bottles at delis, farm shops and wine merchants across our region.

"Most people think of sloe gin in terms of a nip, but all our spirits can be the base for loads of fabulous cocktails," says Andy. "Sloe gin and tonic works very well, and in the summertime strawberry vodka and soda goes down very well.

"Then of course they can be poured over ice-cream, while the blackberry vodka is amazing drizzled over apple crumble."

It doesn't stop there. The spent sloes are sent over to a Leicestershire chocolatier who magics them into fresh cream truffles. Who could possibly resist?

Sloeberry Spirits
MULLED SLOE GIN

The perfect hot toddy. Serves 5-6.

Ingredients

500ml cloudy apple juice

400ml cranberry juice

100ml red grape juice

2 lemon slices

3 orange slices

3 cardamom pods

3 star anise

3 cloves

2 cinnamon sticks

A vanilla pod – cut along its length

½ tsp allspice

25ml Melton Mowbray Sloe Gin (per glass)

To garnish – slice of orange and a cinnamon stick per glass

Method

Put all the ingredients, except the sloe gin into a saucepan, cover, and simmer on a low heat for at least 25 to 35 minutes.

Pour 25ml of sloe gin into a hot toddy glass, and top-up with your mulling liquid.

Garnish with a slice of orange and/or a cinnamon stick. For something sweeter add a little sugar while simmering the liquid.

STRAWBERRY SURPRISE

Simple and fun, great for sunny summer afternoons. Serves 6.

Ingredients

350ml Melton Mowbray Vodka & Strawberry

300ml cream soda

100ml soda

Strawberries and mint to garnish

Method

Add the Melton Mowbray Vodka & Strawberry, cream soda and soda to a pitcher.

Garnish with strawberries and mint.

Serve in a champagne flute with a little ice.

Crafty COFFEE

Coffee roastery, coffee shop and crafty burgers leading Leicester's craft food revival.

Having a really fine coffee roaster is a boost to any city centre. With St Martin's Tea and Coffee you now get two further brilliant businesses thrown in. With best-in-class burgers in the evenings and an awesome all-day coffee shop, together they are at the very heart of the fine food explosion that is happening around the St Martin's area.

Andy Hall has been building his coffee business over the last decade – importing, roasting, blending and selling a variety of the world's great coffees. The associated coffee shop was doing ok, but things really took off in 2013 when a couple full of ideas for informal dining picked up on Leicester as a city that was going places.

Chef Chris Elliman has a gastropub background in London, but had seen the popularity of the pop-up – an informal, fun, time-limited restaurant that could deliver amazing food at low prices. With Leicestershire ticking all the boxes for outstanding local produce and suppliers, Crafty Burger was launched as a pop-up at St Martin's offering burgers made from a bespoke blend of 28-day aged beef which is ground and hand-pressed everyday on site.

Leicester went mad for it. And for the triple-cooked, hand-cut maris piper fries pimped up with spiced pulled ox cheek and jalapenos, and for the sides like the pigcorn poppers – gorgeous cubes of belly pork in panko crumb with a homemade pineapple and chilli relish – and for the craft beers from brewers Purity. We just loved it all.

The partnership between Andy Hall and Chris and his wife Andrea was such a success that Crafty not just came back as a permanent evening fixture from Thursday to Saturday, but they joined the business and relaunched the daytime coffee shop with a new kitchen too. With Andrea winning plaudits for a great front-of-house operation, Chris and his team provide some of the most classy café food in the region – from vegan treats like baba ganoush sprinkled with pomegranate jewels to incredible Indonesian curries from Javan chef Bobby Ananta.

Crafty also continues to evolve with the early 2016 menu introducing the likes of tempura soft-shell crab and a "Crafty Mess" gelato made for them by their neighbours at Gelato Village.

"We're independent and individual," says Andrea. "We go the extra mile and people really respond. We're so pleased we've got this great partnership and so pleased we chose Leicester."

St Martin's Tea & Coffee

BOBBY'S OX CHEEK RENDANG WITH ROASTED PINEAPPLE & CUCUMBER SALAD

A spicy, deeply flavoured Indonesian curry. Serves 6.

Ingredients

8 shallots

5 garlic cloves

6 red chillies, large

4cm fresh ginger

2 tbsp vegetable oil

1 lemongrass stalk

5 cloves

6 ox cheeks, cut into large chunks

1 tsp ground white pepper

2cm tamarind pulp

50g coconut or white sugar

3 bay leaves

500ml coconut milk

5-10 tbsp grated coconut (frozen is fine)

½ tsp cumin

1 tbsp coriander seeds

For the pineapple salad

1 pineapple, peeled and sliced lengthways and dusted with soft brown sugar

Half a cucumber, diced

Juice and zest of one lime

Sliced chilli, toasted peanuts and spring onion to garnish

Method

This was the first dish Bobby cooked in the St Martin's kitchen on his trial shift - he was hired immediately! The conversion of collagen to gelatin is vital to the dish's success; when the ox cheek is wobbly not firm, it is ready.

Take the sugar-dusted pineapple and caramelise in a dry frying pan on a medium heat. When cooled chop in to small 2cm chunks. Add the cucumber dice, lime juice and zest and set aside.

Whizz the shallots, garlic, chillies and ginger into a food processor, blend to make into a paste, then set aside.

Heat the oil in a large casserole dish, add the lemongrass and cloves, curry paste and beef. Add 2 litres water, then cook on a low heat for about two hours.

Add the pepper, tamarind, salt, coconut, bay leaves and coconut milk.

Fry the grated coconut, cumin and coriander seeds until golden, then grind. Add to the pan and cook for 2 hours on a really low heat, stirring occasionally. Serve with steamed fragrant rice and pineapple salad.

Garnish with sliced chilli, toasted peanuts and spring onions.

St. Martin's Tea & Coffee
FARMYARD JAM BURGER

A gooey cheese and bacon burger with a sweet and sour twist. Serves 4.

Ingredients

500g good quality minced beef with about 20% fat, loosely formed in to four tennis ball sized patties

8 thin rashers smoked streaky bacon

4 Red Leicester slices

4 brioche burger buns (available from good bakers and supermarkets)

For the maple and bacon jam

20g unsalted butter

50g smoked pancetta cubes

1 large white onion, sliced

1 tbsp tomato purée

1 tbsp soft light brown sugar

2 tbsp maple syrup

A good splash of Worcestershire sauce

For the burger sauce

1 tbsp minced gherkin

1 tbsp ketchup

1 tbsp mayonnaise

1 tbsp French's American mustard

For the garnish

1 red onion, sliced

1 baby gem lettuce, washed and separated

Gherkins, sliced – to taste

Method

Making a good burger is not about being a great cook; it's 20% preparation and having everything to hand (they cook very quickly!), 60% sourcing good quality ingredients and 20% technique. The good news is that you can make everything in advance and throw it all together last minute.

The beef is important; you want a good quality mince with a fair bit of fat running through it. At Crafty we grind dry aged chuck ourselves and loosely form the patties. The reason for the light handling of the patty is that it results in the juices and fat filling the air pockets and staying in the burger rather than dripping in to the pan. Once your patties are formed, cover in cling film and refrigerate for at least 3 hours to firm up.

Next prepare the maple and bacon jam. In a saucepan add the butter over a medium heat and cook the pancetta until it starts to brown. Add the onions and sweat off until they soften and darken (a good half hour). Add the brown sugar, tomato purée, maple syrup and a splash of Worcester sauce. Cook until most of the liquid evaporates. Set aside.

Make the burger sauce by mixing together the ingredients.

Grill both sides of the rashers of smoked streaky bacon until the fat is uniformly golden in colour. Allow them to cool, you should be able to snap them (resist eating them, if you can).

To cook the burger, heat a heavy bottomed pan until smoking. Carefully add your patties and squash on to the pan with a spatula; this enables an even caramelisation of the burger. Season liberally with salt. After 3-5 minutes, juice should start to appear through the middle of the burger. Flip it and season the other side. Add a spoon of bacon jam and a slice of Red Leicester to the patty. Splash some water in the pan and cover with a lid, this starts to steam the cheese.

Toast the bun, spread the burger sauce on the top (and bottom if you like), followed by the lettuce, gherkin and red onion.

The burger is cooked when it is firm to the touch, or 70ºc if you're using a meat thermometer. Allow it to rest on a plate for a couple of minutes before adding to the bun.

Eat and enjoy (with plenty of napkins!)

The lord of THE PIES

Over 190 years of baking make Walker's a genuine Leicester institution.

Talk to any Leicester person of a certain age and they are likely to go misty-eyed at the memory of queueing up outside Walker's Cheapside store at Christmas to make sure they got their pork pie.

Walker's pies are now sold in supermarkets and delis across the land and the Cheapside flagship shop reopened in 2013 complete with a deli counter, meaning new generations are able to pick up a pie, along with sausages and delicious hot food to either enjoy on site or take away.

Walker's was started by Mark Walker on High Street in 1820. At first they made sausages, but soon built a bakery and eventually gained an even bigger reputation for their pork pies. They use the same recipe to this day and the same traditional method of making pork stock for the essential jelly, along with 100 per cent British pork.

In 2015 Walker's range of pies picked up 25 national awards including a Grocer Food and Drink Award and a Great Taste Award. So far in 2016 they have celebrated four Class Champion awards and five Highly Commended titles at the British Pie Awards. These included a Victorian Corset Pork

and Chicken Pie, winner of the speciality pie category "Fit for a Queen" to mark the Queen's 90th birthday.

That's a source of pride to Walker's master pie maker Ian Heircock, but not a surprise: "Our pies are without doubt the best pies in the country and of course I can say that because I've been lovingly making them for the last 38 years," he said with a smile. "Our pies are traditionally baked in a fluted hoop as opposed to a tin or freestanding to retain the richness in the pastry case. We are proud and passionate about our pies and are thrilled to be celebrating another successful year of awards."

Ian is a hard-working ambassador for the pie, known to many for the pie-making classes he has run for groups.

Walker & Son remains a Leicestershire-owned business, part of the Melton-based Samworth Brothers, along with fellow pie-makers Dickinson and Morris.

So there's a great history and a booming presence for this famous name, manufacturers of a true Leicester legend.

Walker's Pies
CHICKEN, BACON & RED WINE WITH BAKED SUET CRUST

A hearty pie from Walker and Sons master pie maker Ian Heircock.

Ingredients

For the pastry

488g plain flour

14g salt

1g baking powder

115g lard

207ml cold water

174g beef suet, chilled to 12ºc

For the filling

720g roast chicken, diced

40g onion, diced

120g smoked bacon lardons

140g silverskin onions

180g mushrooms, sliced

8g salt

2g black pepper

32g tomato purée

10g chicken stock cube

4g garlic

160ml red wine

60g roux (30g each of flour and butter mixed)

2g malt extract

2g paprika

450ml vegetable stock

180ml water

2 sprigs thyme

20ml rapeseed oil

Egg wash

Method

For the pastry, mix together the flour, salt and baking powder, then add lard and rub in.

Add the water and mix to form a paste, then gently fold in the chilled suet, leaving the suet visible. Wrap in cling film and store in the fridge until the filling is made (a little tip – a good pastry cleans its own bowl!).

For the filling, heat the rapeseed oil and fry the onions until soft, then add the garlic and cook for one minute. Add the water, vegetable stock, crumbled chicken stock cube, salt, black pepper, paprika, malt extract, tomato puree and bring to the boil. Then add the bacon lardons and simmer for 3 minutes, the silverskin onions for a further 2 minutes, then mushrooms for a further 2 minutes and finally stir in the flour and butter roux to thicken. Add the red wine and thyme, bring back to boil and simmer for one minute.

Turn off the heat and add the chicken, stirring slowly. Cover and place in fridge.

When you are ready to bake, take the pastry out of the fridge and let it warm up for 10 minutes. Roll out two-thirds of the pastry to about 5mm and line a pie foil or foils depending on the size you want. Fill the pastry shells to around two-thirds and roll the remaining pastry to about 3mm and adhere the lid to the pastry base, trim any excess and crimp the edges.

Egg wash the lid and place on a baking tray in a pre-heated oven at 180°c for around 30 minutes, making sure the pastry is golden brown.

Award-winning BUTCHERS

High quality traditional butchers with top awards for everything from pork pies to their training scheme.

There's something about a quality independent retailer that has been going for over 130 years. You know that they are not going to throw away that hard-won reputation for a quick buck.

Walter Smith's butchers date back to the 1870s when young Walter left Cambridgeshire to seek his fortune in Birmingham. His butchery in the Jewellery Quarter thrived and today the business that bears his name has branches across the Midlands, including at the Woodlands Garden Centre in Stapleton, near Hinckley.

"We have strong traditional values," says director Robert Jones. "We source locally and we source the best we can find. The vast majority of our products are made on the premises, from our award-winning sausages to home-cured bacon and gourmet dishes to go."

The latter, such as chicken breasts with a lemon, ginger and lime marinade, have proved especially popular with time-poor younger consumers. "The horsemeat scandal was the best possible advert for quality butchers," says Robert. "With our ready meals you know you get high quality, locally sourced meat."

There's been no shortage of awards for Walter Smith products but the one that really makes them glow with pride is Supreme Champion from the Great Taste Awards for their pork pie.

"When I was a trainee butcher I noticed people always had pickle or sauce or something with a pork pie," says Robert. "I thought 'if they have to add something, there must be something missing!' I wanted to come up with a pie with a flavour profile so strong it didn't need anything else."

He looked back into the company's records and after some four years of development settled on uncured meat from the shoulder and belly, a hot water pastry given a firm crust with a touch of Demerara sugar and the company's own top-secret gelatin recipe. The result beat off some 4,500 entries to be the acclaimed the very best food item in the foodie 'Oscars'.

"We continue to sell hundreds of them from our Leicestershire shop," beams Robert.

Another thing that sets Walter Smith apart is their commitment to training the next generation of skilled butchers. In 2014 they were named best training scheme in the UK by the Meat Trades Council and young apprentice Chris Riley of the Leicestershire shop was named Britain's Young Butcher of the Year.

"We're proud to be meat specialists," concludes Robert Jones. "And we aspire to be the very best in the UK."

Walter Smith

Walter Smith
AWARD WINNING BUTCHERS AND FARMERS SINCE 1885

Walter Smith Fine Foods
CHICKEN CHASSEUR

Getting a good chicken makes all the difference. At Walter Smith we stock a large range of poultry and for that special occasion we'd recommend the finest free range Packington chickens from Alex Mercer.

Ingredients

4 good sized chicken legs

2 tbsp olive oil

6 shallots, coarsely sliced

250g mushrooms

1 tbsp tomato purée

300ml white wine

400ml beef or chicken stock

3-4 large tomatoes, quartered and deseeded

Sprinkling fresh tarragon leaves and chopped parsley

Salt and pepper for seasoning

Method

Season the chicken with the salt and pepper and heat the olive oil in a lidded sauté pan or shallow casserole dish. Pan-fry the chicken over a medium-high heat, turning until golden on both sides. Remove from the pan and keep to one side. Drain off the majority of excess fat left in the pan as you will only need about two tablespoons in the pan to cook the shallots and mushrooms.

Return the pan to the heat and add the shallots and mushrooms, stir intermittently until they are beginning to soften and have taken some colour, usually about 6-8 minutes.

Now add the white wine and tomato purée followed by the stock whilst gently stirring continuously. Now return the chicken to the pan and bring ingredients to a simmer.

Place a lid on the pan and continue to let the ingredients simmer for about an hour or until the chicken is tender and cooked through. To finish, allow the ingredients to cool slightly in the pan so you can skim off any excess fat which settles at the surface before adding the tomatoes. Finally simmer without the lid for an additional 3-4 minutes to soften the tomatoes before scattering over the chopped tarragon and parsley.

Walter Smith Fine Foods
HOW TO SELECT AND COOK THE PERFECT STEAK

To achieve the perfect steak eating experience we have to start at the most important part of the process – the steak!

At Walter Smith our sirloin and rib-eye steaks are dry-aged in our specialist dry-ageing cabinets. Dry-ageing beef for 21-28 days will lose 30% of moisture from the muscle, this then creates a greater concentration of beef flavour and depth of taste, and ultimately this process lends to a superior tender eating steak.

Cooking the steak

Remove the steak from the fridge 1-2 hours before cooking and allow to reach room temperature.

We recommend a heavy duty thick based griddle pan, preferably non-stick.

Place the griddle pan on a high heat.

Oil the steak lightly all over.

At the last moment before placing in to the pan season with salt and pepper.

Place the steaks into the pan, turning each minute to ensure an even cook.

Do not overload the pan, only cook two steaks at a time.

With a pair of tongs hold the steak and brown the sides.

We recommend the following cooking times for a 2cm thick sirloin or rib eye.

Blue 1 minute each side

Rare 1 minute 30 seconds each side

Medium Rare 2 minutes each side

Medium 2 minutes 30 seconds each side

Well done 4 minutes each side

Tip:

Remember to rest your steak for at least five minutes.

The steak will absorb the free running juices resulting in a moist and tender steak.

Brewing in
LEICESTERSHIRE

The beating heart of the UK
brewing scene, Leicestershire is
undoubtedly a beer enthusiast's
dream destination.
From micro to massive,
bottles to barrels, the region
is positively teeming with
knowledgeable, forward thinking
producers – offering a wide range
of stunning ales.
Here, we take a look at
the finest...

Experience COUNTS

Ambitious young brewery with a thoroughly professional set up.

The vast majority of micro-breweries start from enthusiastic homebrewers following their passion and scaling up to commercial kit. They produce quality beer, though they also find out how difficult it can be to get into the supply chains of the big pub companies.

Loughborough's Charnwood Brewery is a rather different beast. Director Andrew Reed had some 15 years experience as Sales Director with Lincolnshire brewers Batemans. His detailed knowledge led him to think there was a real gap in the market for an independent, local brewer in the Charnwood and Soar Valley area.

In late 2014 they set up as a family business with wife Andrea supplying the brewing expertise, having been trained by industry legend Sara Barton of Brewster's Brewery. One year on they are a ten-barrel microbrewery working at full capacity and producing some 11,000 pints a week.

They have two regular brews – the light, refreshing Salvation at 3.8% and the 4% best bitter Vixen, with its hints of honey, spice and hedgerow fruits. These have been supplemented by monthly special brews, which are being repeated in 2016, alongside many new ones. These include their SIBA award winner, American Pale Ale.

"We brew beers we want to drink and that are going to sell," says Andrew. "We've all had beers that are too strong or too strongly flavoured and a half is probably enough. I like to think I know what sells and when it sells and, so far, it's working and we have sold everything we produce. In early 2016 we've expanded production capacity by 30 per cent and we think we'll sell all that too."

The business is permanently supplying some 30 local pubs, clubs and shops with draught and bottled beers. They also have their own thriving shop and bar where customers can sit and see the brewery process happening as they sip the product. The brewery has also linked up with a local artisan baker who uses their yeast to bake popular loaves on sale at the brewery.

"Consistent quality is everything," says Andrew. "We like to think our branding is strong, but while branding might get you your first sale, it's quality that will give you repeat sales."

"I think we've quickly established a really good local business for the Charnwood and Soar Valley areas," he adds. "Our challenge now is to establish ourselves across Leicestershire."

Charnwood Brewery

Fifth generation
BREWERS

Family-owned business that has stayed passionate about beer and about Leicestershire.

When William Everard opened his Leicester brewery in 1849 he no doubt did so with the confidence typical of his fellow Victorian entrepreneurs. But one doubts he ever imagined that his company would become synonymous with Leicester for well over 165 years and that the fifth generation of his family would still chair the business.

So how has Everards ridden out the great tectonic shifts that have convulsed the brewing industry over the last fifty years? Great beers are important obviously, but that's not always been enough for others. The strong regional identity has helped – Everard's iconic Tiger bitter, for example, is named in honour of the Royal Leicestershire Regiment which got the Tigers nickname from its time in India, a name which also transferred to City's rugby team.

What has also been key is a positive, supportive approach to pub management at a time when "pubco" has become a byword for rapaciousness. "We own all our pubs but all our licensees get a three year landlord and tenant protected tenancy agreement," says Erika Hardy, Head of Marketing. "We support them in whatever they need, giving them the freedom to run the kind of pub they want to run."

For some, such as The Queen's Head in Saddington, that means developing a high quality food offer.

Everards' four core beers – Beacon, Tiger, Original and Sunchaser – are supplemented by monthly special brews. "This is such an exciting time for brewing right now and we've a passionate brewing team with tremendous depth of knowledge," says Erika. "Right now they are working on a Mad Hatter's ale that will be flavoured with apple and rosehip tea – I know they are going to make a great tasting pint."

The company displays a commendably collegiate approach to their brewing and regularly host guest brewers from around the world. With their celebrated Gold Course they actually get their licensees to come in and brew themselves, the results of which sometimes make it to the pumps. They even go into partnerships with competitor microbreweries through Project William, a scheme which helps small scale brewers to get their own pubs in exchange for an Everards pump on the bar.

The company has around 180 pubs in 14 counties, predominantly in the East Midlands. "Having a strong presence locally is very important to us," concludes Erika. "Our heart is very much in Leicestershire."

Everards Brewery

Everards Brewery
SLOW-BRAISED PORK BELLY
IN TIGER BITTER

Hearty pork dish with a jus of Leicestershire's finest plus apple fritters, apple purée and spring onion mash cake. Serves 2.

Ingredients

4 rashers pork belly

2 pints Everards Tiger bitter

2 medium potatoes, washed and chopped

1 star anise

Olive oil

Salt

Pepper

Splash milk

2 knobs butter (or as needed)

1 egg, beaten

1 spring onion, finely chopped

3 slices of streaky bacon (for garnish if you wish)

2 red apples (one peeled and diced, one cored and sliced)

1 clove garlic, chopped

Splash of water

227g savoy cabbage

175ml of red wine

1 bay leaf

Breadcrumbs

Rosemary

Cornflour

Method

Preheat oven to 200°c. Put the pork belly into a deep oven dish, half cover with Tiger bitter and red wine, season with salt and pepper. Do not cover the pork as you want the pork belly skin to crisp up. Add star anise and bay leaf to taste, braise for 1¾ hours.

Meanwhile, boil the potatoes until tender, then drain and mash them with the milk and butter, season and stir in the spring onions. Spread the mash onto a chopping board and using a large scone cutter, cut 4 mash circles about 1cm thick to form the potato cake. Brush the tops with beaten egg. Set aside the remaining egg.

After the pork belly has braised for 1¾ hours, take pork belly out, and place on a baking tray, add potato cake to the tray and bake for another 15 to 20 minutes until golden brown and the pork belly skin is crisp.

To make the sauce, reduce the Tiger bitter stock by three quarters then add butter and cornflour to thicken and put aside for service.

In a saucepan add diced apple, a knob of butter, a little oil and seasoning (you can add rosemary if you wish), garlic, a splash of water and cook over a light heat until soft, then mash apples into a purée.

To make the apple fritters, dip the sliced apples into the remaining beaten egg, shake off excess, then press into breadcrumbs, chill until needed, then deep fry until golden brown.

To prepare the cabbage, cut into strips, melt some butter in a saucepan over a light heat, add the cabbage and a good splash of water, wilt down with a lid on the pan until cooked - this should be about 5 minutes.

Reheat the sauce, check seasoning, take the pork belly and potato cake out of oven. Assemble dish with two pork belly slices in the middle of the plate, potato cake and a dollop of cabbage on the side, apple purée on top of one of the pork slices, sauce round the plate and rosemary garnish.

Tip

To make the dish easier, you can prepare the potato cakes, apple purée and apple fritters in advance.

Word of MOUTH

Fine ales from the heart of Leicestershire.

For many years they almost disappeared. But now, they are back and they are thriving – passionate little craft breweries that knock out tremendous ales, tailored to local taste, celebrating their local communities and doing it in a sustainable fashion on a human scale.

The Langton Brewery is just such a one. Their range of beers go down a storm with drinkers, not only in the villages of their home turf of South Leicestershire but extending into Nottinghamshire, Northamptonshire and Rutland.

It's a labour of love from former publican Alistair Chapman and colleague David Dyson, originally a precision engineer. Alistair had been licensee of The Bell at East Langton, where he first started a microbrewery in the outbuildings. When he sold the pub the new owner wasn't interested in continuing it, but fortunately the friends decided to see if the brewery business could stand on its own.

They moved it a couple of miles to a friend's farm. David trained in the brewing process and discovered he had a real skill for it, creating beers of great consistency and clarity - to such a degree that their Inclined Plane, the hoppy, straw-coloured ale named after the local landmark at Foxton Locks, won the Bronze Award in the best bitter category in the Champion Beer of Great Britain Awards in 2014.

Inclined Plane and the session bitter, Caudle, remain the core of their range but over the last decade Langton have made some 50 brews, most of them named after aspects of rural life. For example, Caudle is named after the hills which surround their local villages, Bowler was created for the local cricket club, while Woodsman was named after a local 'character'.

The business remains at the heart of its community, from offering personalised bottles to their popular brewery tours and now an annual beer and music festival. That's in addition to using spent brewing grain to feed local cattle, hops for prime garden mulch and even water to irrigate Christmas trees on their host farm. Their beers are also to be found in specially made chutneys and sausages.

It's a joy to uncover a business that has had so little to do with some finely-honed marketing strategy. "Basically we've grown through word of mouth," says Alistair, "We put this down to producing quality products with excellent customer service."

Highly
RECOMMENDED

An independent store run by a team with a passion for helping people explore new wines.

"It's really exciting when after recommending a wine to someone, they come back and want more," says Duncan Murray. "When they tell us this was so much nicer than whatever they drank before – we get a real kick out of that."

Duncan's shop in the centre of Market Harborough typifies what is best about independent retailing. It's not just that you get knowledgeable and helpful service, with specialist advice in areas such as wine and food pairing, it's that you know you have left behind the world of anodyne, lowest common denominator wines.

"We only sell what we like here," Duncan emphasises. "There's a buying team of three and we'll only stock it if it gets at least two out of three votes."

Duncan thanks his grandparents for his love of wine, but it was a college trip to the French vineyards that turned it into a career. Talking with the owners of the legendary Chateau Figeac in St Émilion he realised this was a far more interesting world than that promised by his studies. The next decade was spent learning the trade by working at wine retailers Oddbins and in vineyards across France.

Eventually in 2001 he and his wife Megan felt they wanted to go it alone with a shop that just sold interesting, characterful wines. His team are always looking for small independent producers you won't find in the big retailers.

They now have something of a southern European specialism – so much so that it even closes in the afternoons for a siesta. "I think we may be the only shop in northern Europe to do that!" grins Duncan.

"We prefer areas with eclectic, quirky grape varieties. More and more people are looking for something with a bit of pizzazz and we can help them. We've found some fabulous wines from areas such as Sicily and Greece."

As well as the compelling retail offer, Duncan is in big demand to supply restaurants and run tastings and masterclasses for local clubs and societies. The shop is shortly to expand to give customers more space and hopefully in the future a state of the art wine-tasting dispensing machine.

Compact, bijou, eclectic – this is a shop for those looking to expand their horizons.

Wine MATCHING

We asked Duncan Murray Wines to come up with a wine match for the recipes in this book so you can be sure to have the perfect accompaniment. All the wines are available at Duncan's shop in Market Harborough.

BEAUTIFUL PUBS COLLECTIVE
Duck Rillettes

Sauternes de Rayne Vigneau (Bordeaux, France) - £25
Hand-harvested grape by grape to pick just the best ones giving a rich yet refreshing white with sweet, baked apple, peach, apricot and notes of sultana which will pick up beautifully with the rillettes.

Duck Egg Scotch Egg

Famille Perrin Luberon White (Provence, S. France) - £10
Luberon is the area made famous by Peter Mayle's stories of ex-pat life in rural southern France where the grapes Bourboulenc, Grenache Blanc, Ugni Blanc and Roussanne make a fresh yet full flavour.

THE BERKELEY ARMS
Braised Shoulder of Venison

Appassimento Edizione Oro (Veneto, NE Italy) - £14
Made from late harvested super ripe grapes making a rich and raisiny dry red (not unlike a Valpolicella Ripasso in style) with spice, chocolate and vanilla notes on top of the heady black fruits.

THE BEWICKE ARMS
Herb Crusted Haunch of Venison, Pressing of Root Vegetables

Medievo Gran Reserva Rioja (Rioja, N. Spain) - £20
This blend of Tempranillo, Mazuelo and Graciano grape varieties is seductively fulsome yet complex and elegant with smoky flavours of ripe red berry and cherry fruits plus sweet spice. A Rioja of this calibre will add lustre to the richness of the herb crusted haunch.

BRADGATE PARK VENISON
Venison Casserole

Chateau du Vieux Parc Selection Rouge Corbières (Languedoc, S. France) - £14
Amazingly good value, full-flavoured red in the style of a Châteauneuf-du-Pape made by Louis Panis, one of our favourite twinkly eyed producers in the deep south of France and the wine cries out for fulsome flavoured dishes like his wife's wild boar or this super casserole.

Keeper's Pie

Du Clos Coteaux du Languedoc (S. France) - £9
A cheeky little red made by an English chum in the Languedoc, this is intense and concentrated yet fruity and elegant and brims with plummy fruits of the forest flavours.

MAS DE BOISLAUZON

MAS DE BOISLAUZON

MAS
DE
BOISLAUZON

CÔTES DU RHÔNE VILLAGES

MAS
DE
BOISLAUZON

CÔTES DU RHÔNE VILLAGES

CAPEZZANA

di Capezzana

Carmignano

D.O.C.G.

2012

Mas de Boislauzon Côtes
du Rhône Villages

COCOA AMORE
Smoked Mackerel Ganache on Cocoa, Porter and Treacle Bread
Gewurztraminer René Muré (Alsace, E. France) - £16

I like to think of the Muré family as the French side of the Murray family. The Muré family have been making wine in southern Alsace since the end of the 30 Years War in 1648; we think they've finally cracked it as you get rose petal, lychee and gingerbread spice in this elegant quaffer.

DELI AT 58
Colston Bassett and Spring Onion Scones
Guntrum Riesling Kabinett Nierstein Bergkirche (Rheinhessen, Germany) - £13

An elegant and classical Riesling scent paired with aromas of tropical fruits. Green apple, citrus, pineapple and melon. Minerally fresh notes of apple, honey and cream lead to a palate of such excellence I thought I'd died and gone to heaven.

DICKINSON AND MORRIS
Homemade Melton Mowbray Pork Pie
Ciconia Tinto (Alentejo, S. Portugal) - £10

Combining approachability with southern Portugal's most likeable features of rich soft dark berry fruit with a smidge of roast and dried fruit notes; this red is unoaked, and doesn't need or want for it, but what it does want is PIE and lots of it!

EVERARDS
Slow-Braised Pork Belly in Tiger Bitter
Quinta do Portal Colheita Tinto (Douro, N. Portugal) - £14

To be recommended to those who love red Bordeaux but have been priced out of the market, this full flavoured red has smooth tannins and lots of cherry, blackberry and spice and is a sublime pairing for pork which itself is a staple of the Portuguese diet.

FARNDON FIELDS
Dauphinoise Potatoes
Chateau du Vieux Parc Selection Blanc Corbières (Languedoc, SE France) - £14

An opulent mix of Grenache Blanc, Roussanne and Vermentino; this tastes similar to white Châteauneuf-du-Pape being full flavoured yet fresh, is lighter on the purse and very quaffable with rich dishes.

THE FOX AND HOUNDS
Monkfish with Madras, Vermouth and Granny Smith Velouté
Domaine du Poujol Pico Blanc (Languedoc, SE France) - £10

Made by an Anglo-American husband and wife team, this blend of Vermentino, Roussanne and Carignan Blanc is vibrant, fresh and elegant, with honeyed apricot and rich citrus flavours plus minerally notes. The lightly spiced monkfish will be beautifully complemented by this adaptable wine.

Milly's Salad
Tinpot Hut Marlborough Sauvignon Blanc (New Zealand) – £14

A complex and elegant wine with intense aromas of blackcurrant bush, crushed lemongrass and thyme. The flavours of passion fruit, juicy melon and gooseberry will be a marvel with Milly's dish.

JAMES' CAFE BISTRO
Lemon Torte with Strawberry and Honey Sorbet
Domaine Jones Muscat Petits Grains (Roussillon, S. France) - £17

Originally from Ashby de la Zouch, Katie Jones moved to Cathar country in Languedoc-Roussillon over 20 years ago and she now has a small vineyard making this utterly delicious, sweet and floral muscat with mouth-watering honeysuckle, exotic Turkish delight and fresh elderflower flavours.

JOHN'S HOUSE
Bradgate Park Fallow Deer, Smoked Beetroot, Quince and Chocolate
Predator Old Vine Zinfandel (California, USA) - £20

Full bodied and fulsome in flavour it possesses astounding flavours of smoky and spicy dark and red fruits, together with rich herbs and notes of smoked, spicy ham. This deliciously sumptuous red wine will be stunning with both the fallow deer and smoked beetroot, as well as complement the richness of the quince and chocolate.

KAYAL
Chemmeen Kootu
Gocker Pinot Gris (Alsace, E. France) - £13

Asian cuisine and Alsace wines are a match made in heaven, so big thanks to Bacchus, the Roman god of wine. This Pinot Gris has aromas of mulling spices, honey, lychee and apple strudel; it is intense, fresh and dry with lots of baked apple flavour.

MARQUESS OF EXETER

Pan Fried Fillet of Red Snapper with Roasted Red Pepper, Spring Onion & Ginger Salsa

Casa Silva Reserva Viognier – (Colchagua Valley, Chile) - £12

These chaps are Chile's most awarded winery of this century and no surprise as this tastes like a mini Condrieu (one of the Rhône valley's most gorgeous white wines) having bags of personality with notes of nut, peach and apricot yet is beautifully fresh and lovely.

MATTHEW O'CALLAGHAN

Melton Empanadas

La Flor Malbec (Mendoza, Argentina) - £12

Intense yet elegant with loads of spice, blackberry, plum and raspberry jam flavours, you can see why Malbec has become the signature grape of Argentina; this is a dangerously easy glugger.

ODD JOHN'S

Duo of Bradgate Venison

Les Volcans Syrah Puy de Dôme (Loire, France) - £14

The high altitude volcanic soils of the Loire valley near Clermont Ferrand produce a full bodied spicy red with the complex flavours one would expect from a Cote Rôtie of the Rhône valley which lies two sets of hills to the east on exactly the same latitude.

Simon's Little Tart

Guntrum Auslese Riesling Oppenheim Herrenberg (Rheinhessen, Germany) - £17

Tropical fruit flavours with a delicate sweetness; this is fresh and light with a nudge of gooseberry and baked apple that won't overpower the lemon tart. A lovely wine with wide appeal.

Pork and Tarragon Terrine with Burleigh's Gin and Apple Jelly

Casa Silva Late Harvest Semillon Gewürztraminer ½ bottle (Colchagua Valley, Chile) - £9

Of course you could partner this dish with a Burleighs gin and tonic but our cool climate dessert wine from Chile will work equally well with its pink grapefruit and orange notes, this is a heavenly number displaying lychees and peaches and is really rather dangerous!

THE OLD BULLS HEAD

Prawn and crab linguine

Pipoli Fiano-Greco (Basilicata, S. Italy) - £11

The roots of both grape varieties go back to Roman times so they are perfect for a toga party! This is a fresh and fruity little number with a nose of blossom and tropical fruit (from the Fiano) and apple, lemon and honey (from the Greco).

Venison steak with fondant potato and chocolate jus

Casa Silva Reserva Carmenere (Colchagua Valley, Chile) - £12

Carmenere has become one of the noble red wine grapes of Chile, having originally emigrated from Bordeaux, France. This example is dark, rich, full bodied and full of juicy, ripe, spicy dark fruits such as blackberry and plum. The wine's ripe tannins will complement both the steak and the chocolate jus.

PADDY'S MARTEN INN

Jinga Masti

Amalaya Torrontes-Riesling (Salta, Argentina) - £11

An aromatic roller-coaster ride, reminiscent of an Alsace white with turbo-charged Argentinian attitude; citrus, peach and grapefruit-a-go-go! The tropical fruits work superbly with spicy dishes without either overpowering the other.

Slow-Cooked Lamb on the Bone Curry

Primitivo Visconti (Puglia, S. Italy) - £10

Primitivo, while native to the heel of Italy, is possibly more well known as Zinfandel and this medium bodied red is smooth, tangy and juicy with spice, pepper and deep dark fruit flavours and a lick of vanilla to cope with the spice of the dish without being overbearing.

Langton Fox Lager (Thorpe Langton, Leicestershire) - £2.50

Well it wouldn't be right if we didn't suggest a lager to pair up with this curry. As well as being perfect for supporters of Leicester City it tastes great too, being crisp and refreshing.

QUEEN OF BRADGATE

Shin of Beef Chilli

Sette Vigne Vino Italiano (Italy)- £13

Sette Vigne is a delicious and totally unique red, one of a kind blend of the seven most noble indigenous grape varieties in Italy - from seven of the most important and distinct wine regions in Italy. Full, powerful, velvety… enticing…unforgettable.

THE ROYAL OAK
Applewood Smoked Chicken Bourguignon
Mas d'en Compte Blanco (Priorat, SE Spain) - £25
And now for something completely different! This belter from Barcelona is made like a white Burgundy but from a bonkers mix of grapes and is voluptuous, elegant and mouth-coating with flavours of spiced citrus, fig and apricot with buttery tropical fruit.

RUTLAND CHARCUTERIE
Roasted vegetable and charcuterie board
Santorini Hatzidakis (Santorini, Greece) - £17
Made from Assyrtiko grapes which are native to the volcanic island of Santorini (home to the myth of Atlantis – pop in to the shop to ask us why) this belting white is from high altitude vineyards and is then made in a cave and is full, dry and gorgeously refreshing with complex citrus, stone fruit and brioche flavours that fill the mouth.

ST MARTIN'S TEA AND COFFEE
Ox-cheek Beef Rendang with Roasted Pineapple
Greywacke Pinot Noir (Marlborough, New Zealand) - £32
Created by Kevin Judd, chief winemaker at Cloudy Bay and this is a highly perfumed style featuring exotic fruit sweetness, a cedar-like spiciness and a delicate smoky scent reminiscent of lapsang souchong, while the palate is dense and generous with ripe cherry and plum richness.
Farmyard Jam
Troublemaker (California, USA) - £19
You know who you are; intensely rich, velvety smooth, sneaky good! A Californian take on Châteauneuf-du-Pape made from Syrah, Grenache, Petite Sirah, Zinfandel and Mourvèdre; this combines elegance and power with buckets of dark fruit and spice.

WALKER AND SON
Chicken, Bacon and Red Wine with Baked Suet Crust
Beaujolais Villages Manoir du Carra (Burgundy, France) - £12
An outstanding example of the Gamay grape which is much nicer than many a Fleurie, being much punchier and full flavoured than many expect from Beaujolais. The strawberries and cream notes are both refined and seductive.

WALTER SMITH
Chicken Chasseur
Irancy P-L et J-F Bersan (Burgundy, France) - £18
This Pinot Noir from near Chablis is made by a Leicester Tigers fan; Jean-Francois (or Jef to his mates) Bersan plays fly-half for Auxerre old boys, training night is on a Thursday, however, this usually involves a fair bit of whisky 'tasting!' It is velvety smooth and tasty with fresh and juicy raspberry, blackberry and morello cherry, spice and pepper.
"The Perfect Steak"
Chateau Hauterive Cuvée Prestige (Cahors, SW France) - £13
While Malbec has found a home in Argentina, the vineyards of Cahors are its origins and this also gives many a Bordeaux a run for its money. We describe this as 'Darth Vader in slippers'. It's BIG! Dark berry fruits with hints of leather and spice; it's definitely the Dark Side!

THE WINDMILL
Rare Chateaubriand
Bad Boy Bordeaux (Bordeaux, SW France) - £19
Made in a garage this crowd-pleaser is primarily Merlot from the Saint-Emilion area and has a richness of flavour, tons of blackcurrant and blackberry fruit and mellow tannins; great with red meats.

Chocolate Box
Truffle Chocolate
Cabernet Sauvignon

Tasting... Ripe blackcurrant flavours are complemented by eucalyptus & 'truffle chocolate' hints.

Perfect with... barbecued meat and/or vegetables

£16.99

PUY DE DÔME
'Les Volcans'
SYRAH
Ooo... the plum, fruit cake, blackberry & spice flavours just climb out of the glass.
13.99

Lagar de Macedos
Tinta Roriz, Tinta Francá & others

Tasting... Lagar refers to the large troughs the grapes are trodden in. This wine is then naturally fermented and matured in oak barrels. A full-flavoured labour of love.

Perfect with... wild boar, rich roasts with herbs & slow-cooked vegetables

£28.99

Chocolate Box
Cherry Chocolate
Grenache, Shiraz & Mataro

Tasting... Enjoy a robust & generous body, with aromas & flavours of dark cherry chocolate, rhubarb, & spice.

Perfect with... big roasts, sausages & casseroles

£16.99

The DIRECTORY

These great businesses have supported the making of this book;
please support and enjoy them.

45 West Distillers
45 Distillery and Gin School
The Collection Yard
Bawdon Lodge Farm
Charley Road
Nanpantan
Leicestershire
LE12 9YE
Telephone - 0116 278 8492
45 Bottle Shop and Bar
4a Hotel Street
Leicester
LE1 5AW
Telephone - 0116 262 7336
Website: www.45westdistillers.com
*The company behind Burleighs Gin, with
their own sophisticated bar and shop in the
heart of the city.*

The Beautiful Pubs Collective
The Forge Inn
Main Street
Glenfield
Leicestershire
LE3 8DG
Telephone: 0116 287 1702
Email: inns@ssoosh.co.uk
Website: www.theforgeinn.co.uk
The Rutland and Derby
21 Millstone Lane
Leicester
LE1 5JN
Telephone: 0116 262 3299
Email: rutlandandderby@ssoosh.co.uk
Website: www.therutlandandderby.co.uk
*A pair of pubs, beautiful by name and
nature.*

The Berkeley Arms
59 Main Street
Wymondham
Leicestershire
LE14 2AG
Telephone: 01572 787587
Email: info@theberkeleyarms.co.uk
Website: www.theberkeleyarms.co.uk
*High class food and service at this classic
country dining pub.*

The Bewicke Arms and Hare Pie Cafe
1 Eastgate
Hallaton
Leicestershire
LE16 8UB
Telephone: 01858 555734
Website: www.thebewicke.com
*South Leicestershire pub back to former
glory with innovative and adventurous
food plus a smart café.*

Bradgate Park Trust
Bradgate Park
Newtown Linford
Leicestershire
LE6 0HE
Telephone: 0116 236 2713
Email: sales@bradgatepark.org
Website: www.bradgatepark.org
Superb meat from the Bradgate Park herd.

Charnwood Brewery
22 Jubilee Drive,
Loughborough,
Leicestershire
LE11 5XS
Telephone: 01509 218666
Email: hello@charnwoodbrewery.co.uk
Website: www.charnwoodbrewery.co.uk
*Family run microbrewery combining
brewery industry nous with great beers.*

Cocoa Amore
34 Silver Street
Leicester
LE1 5ET
Telephone: 0116 262 3278
Email: info@cocoa-amore.co.uk
Website: www.cocoa-amore.co.uk
*Award-winning business offering
innovative handmade chocolates
plus chocolate-making workshops.*

Deli at 58
58 Wards End
Loughborough
Leicestershire
LE11 3HB
Telephone: 01509 263275
Email: hello@thedeliat58.co.uk
Website: www.thedeliat58.co.uk
*New deli going the extra mile to find
exciting products from independent
producers.*

Delilah's Fine Food
4 St Martin's
Leicester
LE1 5PL
Telephone: tbc (Nottingham branch:
0115 948 4461)
Email: food@delilahfinefoods.co.uk
Website: www.delilahfinefoods.co.uk
*A former bank building turned into a
stunning delicatessen.*

Dickinson and Morris
Ye Olde Pork Pie Shoppe
10 Nottingham St
Melton Mowbray
Leicestershire
LE13 1NW
Telephone: 01664 482068
Email: dickinsonandmorris@porkpie.
co.uk
Website: www.porkpie.co.uk
*Melton's longest established pork pie
makers.*

Duncan Murray Wines
10 Adam and Eve St
Market Harborough
Leicestershire
LE16 7LT
Telephone: 01858 464935
Email: info@duncanmurraywines.co.uk
Website: www.duncanmurraywines.
co.uk
*An independent store with a passion for
helping people explore new wines.*

Everards
Everards Wine and Brewery Shop
Castle Acres
Narborough
Leicestershire
LE19 1BY
Telephone: 0116 201 4100
Email: shop@everards.co.uk
Website: www.everards.co.uk
*Passionate about beer and about
Leicestershire since 1849.*

Farndon Fields
Farndon Fields Farm
Farndon Road
Market Harborough
Leicestershire,
LE16 9NP
Telephone: 01858 464838
Email: sales@farndonfields.co.uk
Website: www.farndonfields.co.uk
*Award winning farm shop, along with
a farm restaurant voted Britain's best in
2016.*

The Fox and Hounds
19 The Green
Exton
Rutland
LE15 8AP
Tel: 01572 812403
Email: info@afoxinexton.co.uk
Website: www.facebook.com/
foxandhoundsexton
*Stunning 17th century inn with cosy
fireplaces, fine food and stylish bedrooms.*

Gelato Village
2 St Martins Square
Leicester
LE1 5DF
Telephone: 0116 319 2252
Email: ciao@gelatovillage.co.uk
Website: www.gelatovillage.co.uk
*Glorious gelato made the artisan way with
Italian passion and Leicestershire milk.*

**Hambleton Hall and Hambleton
Bakery**
Hambleton Hall
Hambleton
Oakham
Rutland
LE15 8TH
Telephone: 01572 756991
Email: hotel@hambletonhall.com
Website: www.hambletonhall.com
Website: www.hambletonbakery.co.uk
*One of Britain's finest country house hotels,
a Michelin-starred restaurant and the best
bakery in the UK.*

James' Cafe Bistro
5 East Bond Street
Leicester
LE1 4SX
Telephone: 0116 251 3323
Website: Find on facebook James Cafe
Bistro
*Backstreet bistro with a quirky charm and
focus on freshness.*

John's House
139-141 Loughborough Road
Mountsorrel
Leicestershire
LE12 7AR
Telephone: 01509 415569
Email: dine@johnshouse.co.uk
Website: www.johnshouse.co.uk
*Chef John Duffin returns to the family
farm, opens a restaurant, and wins
Leicestershire's only Michelin star.*

Kayal
153 Granby Street
Leicester
LE1 6FE
Telephone: 0116 255 4667
Email: le@kayalrestaurant.com
Website: www.kayalrestaurant.com
Popular and influential Keralan restaurant "where quality meets tradition."

Langton Brewery
Grange Farm
Welham Road
Thorpe Langton
Market Harborough
Leicestershire
LE16 7TU
Telephone: 01858 540116
Email: info@langtonbrewery.co.uk
Website: www.langtonbrewery.co.uk
Fine ales from the heart of Leicestershire.

Leicester Market
Customer Care Centre
Market Place
Leicester
LE1 5HB
Telephone: 0116 223 2371
Website: www.leicestermarket.co.uk
Historic market going through exciting changes but maintaining its role as the city's heartbeat.

The Marquess of Exeter
52 Main Street
Lyddington
nr Uppingham
Rutland
LE15 9LT
Telephone: 01572 822477
Email: info@marquessexeter.co.uk
Website: www.marquessexeter.co.uk
Chef Brian Baker's exceptional restaurant, pub and hotel.

Melton Mowbray Farmers Market
Scalford Road
Melton Mowbray
Leicestershire
LE13 1JY
Telephone: 01664 562971
Email: fm@meltonmowbraymarket.co.uk
Website: www.meltonmowbraymarket.co.uk
Melton's market is mentioned in the Domesday Book and still offers quality, value and a warm welcome.

Odd John and Family Ltd
174 Main Street
Swithland
Leicestershire
LE12 8TJ
Telephone: 01509 890535
Website: www.oddjohn.co.uk
Go-ahead family business with a pub, event venue and homely cafe and deli in beautiful Charnwood.

The Old Bull's Head
134 Main Street
Woodhouse Eaves
Loughborough
Leicestershire
LE12 8RZ
Telephone: 01509 890255
Website: www.theoldbullshead.co.uk
Lively village dining pub with wide ranging and versatile food offer.

Paddy's Marten Inn
98 Martin St
Leicester
LE4 6EU
Telephone: 0116 266 5123
Email: info@paddysmarteninn.co.uk
Website: www.paddysmarteninn.co.uk
Jamie Oliver-approved Indian restaurant with family recipes and an award winning chef.

Queen of Bradgate
97 High Street
Leicester
LE1 4JB
Telephone: 0116 262 3990
Website: www.queenofbradgate.co.uk
Independent spirit, fine beers and casual dining in the heart of Leicester.

The Royal Oak
The Green
Long Whatton
Loughborough
Leicestershire
LE12 5DB
Telephone: 01509 843694
Email: enquiries@theroyaloaklongwhatton.co.uk
Website: www.theroyaloaklongwhatton.co.uk
A stylish North West Leicestershire inn with a growing reputation for great food.

Rutland Charcuterie
Chestnut Farm
The Granary
Wood Lane
Braunston
Rutland
LE15 8QZ
Telephone: 01572 724655
Email: info@rutlandcharcuterie.co.uk
Website: www.rutlandcharcuterie.co.uk
Premium charcuterie made on a Rutland farm.

St Martin's Tea and Coffee
2-6 St Martin's Walk
St Martins Walk
Leicester
LE1 5DG
Telephone: 251 2879
Website: www.stmartinscofee.co.uk
Coffee roasters, adventurous daytime café and the brilliant Crafty Burger by night.

Sloeberry Spirits
Northfield Farm
Whissendine Lane
Cold Overton
Nr. Oakham
Leicestershire
LE15 7QF
Telephone: 01664 738088
Email: info@sloeberryspirits.co.uk
Website: www.sloebarryspirits.co.uk
*Home of Melton Mowbray Sloe Gin and
other hedgerow fruit spirits.*

Walker and Sons
4-6 Cheapside
Leicester
LE1 5EA
Telephone: 0116 251 4126
Website: www.walkerspies.co.uk
*Celebrated pie makers with a big place in
the hearts of Leicester folk.*

Walter Smith Fine Foods
Wyevale Garden Centre
Ashby Road
Stapleton
Leicestershire
LE9 8JE
Telephone: 01455 290955
Website: www.waltersmith.co.uk
*Award winning butchers and farmers
since 1875.*

The Windmill Inn
83 Brook Street
Wymeswold
Loughborough
LE12 6TT
Telephone 01509 881313
Website: www.thewindmillwymeswold.
com
Email: info@thewindmillwymeswold.
com
*Village pub brought back to life with a
varied local and seasonal food offering.*